On the team!

Joshua 24:15

"This book is crucially important because it calls us back to the heart of our faith and mission—love of God, love of neighbor, and love of each other before a watching world. . . . This book is an honest, hopeful call to face our failures, redefine our success metrics, embrace our challenges, and love one another in ways that show the world who Jesus truly is."

—DAVE MARTIN,
Coordinator, Mosaix PDX

"The American church has never really come to terms with our unity in Jesus. . . . Stafford's book is a clarion call to the church of Jesus to return to Jesus so that his dream—for one people of God living and proclaiming the gospel of hope in a polarized and broken world—can be realized in our day and time."

—RICK MCKINLEY,
Lead Pastor, Imago Dei Community

"Stafford reminds us that Christians must hang together or we will certainly hang separately. His call for collaboration is badly needed in a post-Christian society. We must take seriously his call for unity and find ways to work together as the body of Christ. Use Stafford's effort to inspire you to take the intentional steps necessary to become truly one in Christ."

—GEORGE YANCEY,
Professor of Sociology, Baylor University

"As an African American female pastor, I found great comfort and wisdom in Pastor Avery's words. He beautifully weaves together Scripture with our cultural realities to exhort and bring healing to the church, highlighting hope in the midst of heartbreak. Every personal story, observation, and critique points us back to the importance of our relationship with Jesus and one another, serving as an anchor for the church—present and future."

—ASHLEY BELL,
Global & Local Outreach Pastor, Cedar Mill Bible Church

"Avery Stafford is serving the church well by reminding us that while Jesus was on his way to the cross, he stopped to pray for the unity of his disciples. Through that highlight of its importance and the model of the Trinity itself, we learn four rhythms that are important for the church. I think you will be surprised and challenged, as I was, as you wrestle through these concepts while asking yourself, 'Do others know I'm Jesus' disciple as Jesus defined it?'"

—DAVID WHITAKER,
President, Venture Church Network

"I love this book! . . . I view this book as a 'train the trainer' model for kingdom-building pastors. Imagine heading out to regions in the US to equip pastors to apply these concepts in their communities. Work with local coffee shops to host church collaboration meetings. All pastors need a good reason to hang out and drink more coffee. Well done, brother. This book is just the beginning."

—DAN MCCLURE,
former Lead Pastor, First Christian Church Palo Alto

"Stafford's writing is theologically rich and practical every day, just like the faith and the life of discipleship to Jesus he lives every day. Every leader, and really anyone, would benefit greatly from reading this book. It tells how we can seek to engage the heart of God and live out a robust and genuine kingdom faith that seeks unity and collaboration while embracing a God-created diversity and modeling a better way forward for an onlooking world."

—DOMINIC KAN,
Lead Pastor, Missio Community

"Avery may be overly hopeful. Fair warning: he has the humility, biblical clarity, and track record of resiliency that will make you want to join him. His vision for unity and collaboration feels like turning down a street in my neighborhood that I've passed by countless times but have never turned down—I know it's there, but I'm just not sure I've ever truly experienced it. After reading Avery's heart in these pages, I'm compelled to stumble down this unknown block of the bride of Christ being one today. I'm hoping more of us join him."

—TIM OSBORN,
Lead Pastor, Mosaic Church Portland

"Can you imagine a world where the church works together as all the tribes of humanity to tell the good news about Jesus? Avery Stafford can imagine that world. In his thoughtful, theologically sound, and very challenging Trinitarian proposal, he asks believers to imagine collaborating with one another. . . . Are you considering where to go with your ministry? Then you and your leaders must walk through this work and consider how God is calling you to be a part of what he has always been doing."

—STEPHEN MAXWELL,
Worship and Communications Minister,
North Atlanta Church of Christ

"This work is thoroughly undergirded by Trinitarian theology, pastoral wisdom, and bold insight. It is a timely course correction for any of us who by degrees have been captivated by our cultural narratives of individualism, corporate visions of success, and cheap token attempts at woke virtue signaling. Instead, Avery gives us a rich Trinitarian exhortation to live out of our collective family identity with relationships of love rooted in Jesus' gospel."

—MATT BOWEN,
Lead Pastor, Emmaus Church

"I wholeheartedly agree with Pastor Avery Stafford's challenge to pastors and church leaders that we must pursue 'collaboration as a practice of unity.' I recommend *When Collaboration Mirrors the Trinity* to any church leader who desires to build a culture of collaboration within their local church context. Church collaboration is at the heart of Jesus' prayer in John 17 and is the key ingredient in his command to 'go and make disciples.'"

—DOUG BOYD,
Pastor, Parkside Fellowship

"Stafford's writing reveals that he spends quality time in the timeless presence of divinity within the Trinity. His gospel-saturated book calls local churches and pastors to engage in Christ-centered collaboration instead of religious competition and racial contempt. . . . Stafford is right to believe that when churches collaborate through Christ, they are empowered to join the triumphant Christ in his assaulting march upon the collapsing gates of hell."

—JERRY TAYLOR,
Associate Professor, Abilene Christian University

When Collaboration Mirrors the Trinity

When Collaboration Mirrors the Trinity

Leveraging Unity to Bless Our World

AVERY STAFFORD

Foreword by Kevin Palau

WIPF & STOCK · Eugene, Oregon

WHEN COLLABORATION MIRRORS THE TRINITY
Leveraging Unity to Bless Our World

Wipf & Stock
An Imprint of Wipf and Stock Publishers
199 W. 8th Ave., Suite 3
Eugene, OR 97401

www.wipfandstock.com

PAPERBACK ISBN: 978-1-6667-1065-6
HARDCOVER ISBN: 978-1-6667-1066-3
EBOOK ISBN: 978-1-6667-1067-0

NOVEMBER 12, 2021

To Josh Stafford, the greatest kingdom collaborator I have ever known. I dedicate this book to you, Dad. I wish you were here to read it with me. May it honor your legacy and life and ministry. I am forever proud to be your son.

And to every pastor, educator, small-group leader, and community of faith around the world—

I am rooting for you!

The goal is for all of them to become one heart and mind—

Just as you, Father, are in me and I in you,

So they might be one heart and mind with us.

Then the world might believe that you, in fact, sent me.

(John 17:21 MSG)

WORDS PRAYED BY JESUS OF NAZARETH

Contents

List of Tables

Foreword

Unity Mirrored in the Trinity

THE BEAUTIFUL TRUTH OF God revealed as a trinity in eternal, loving relationship is one of the great mysteries of the Christian faith. No metaphor can capture it fully. No finite mind can comprehend it. Yet, as with most beautiful things, a lack of fully "knowing" it intellectually or a failure to explain it to the uninitiated diminishes that beauty for those willing to meditate and explore. And better yet, to experience that loving relationship, as God intends for all of us.

Biblically, we are each, individually, part of the "body of Christ," and for those of us who've grown up as part of a local church, that's a familiar and comforting metaphor. To think that I matter—that God made me with unique gifts and perspectives, that I'm part of something much bigger and impactful—is thrilling! To think that I'm part of the most significant movement in the history of the world is humbling and inspiring. That's the dream of God. That this ragtag collection of imperfect, often petty, and insecure (yet redeemed) individuals would so unite in love and purpose that we'd actually "be" Jesus in this broken world. We, collectively, are the only physical manifestation of Jesus walking and talking on this planet today.

So how are we doing? When you think of the state of unity and collaboration among local congregations of various denominations, ethnicities, ages, and socio-economic groups in your city or town, what comes to mind? I'll admit to being dismayed at times at how far we've fallen from Jesus' prayer that we'd be one as he and the Father are one.

My friend Avery Stafford has given us an important and unique way to think about the local and global church through the lens of the Trinity's loving "unity within diversity." The Trinity mirrors the kind of love that members of the church—the bride of Christ and the body of Christ—should have for each other.

Unity does not mean sameness any more than a body consists of identical parts. It's unity within diversity. The very point is that out of many unique parts, each with its own designed function, it becomes a living organism that can live and operate in the world. What if our metric for success were not only a growing number of individuals encountering and following Christ but also a growing unity and collaboration among local congregations for the greater good of our cities and towns?

Unity and collaboration are beautiful ends in themselves, not simply a means to an end. It's not just about growing our churches or increasing our influence by showing political leaders that we've got numbers. It's about showing the reality that we do love each other! I love it when I see churches and pastors that "get it." Some churches I know have taken their outreach or missions pastor and "given" them to the city to foster collaboration around churches. That kind of vision is catching!

What would our neighborhoods be like if we genuinely rejoiced with those who rejoice and wept with those who weep? Can I genuinely rejoice at the growth of other churches around me? Do I see their success as my success? That's part of what it means to be the body of Christ.

This vision is what we've begun to see—imperfectly, no doubt—in our home city of Portland, Oregon. Avery and I share the privilege of living in Beaverton, a suburb of Portland. In 2007, a group of perhaps fifty pastors and leaders met to pray and ask the following question: "What more could we do to unite around sharing the good news in our city?" We recognized that in a proudly progressive, radically unchurched place like Portland, where many of our friends and neighbors are quite clear about why they don't go to church, business as usual wasn't going to work. We realized that for many, their perception was of a Christian community deeply divided over belief and practice, political leanings, and theology. The church had become far more known for what it was against than what it was for. Many wouldn't have a clue if asked, "What's the value of the church to our region?"

We were led to some pretty simple conclusions. We needed to collaborate around both serving our community and sharing the good news. We started by going to see our mayor. We went with a humble posture. "Mr. Mayor, we're embarrassed that we've not built a stronger relationship with you and other city leaders over the years. We'd like to change that. If we could raise up thousands of volunteers to serve our community, in partnership with you and other civic leaders, what sorts of projects could we focus on?" From more than two hundred local churches, many thousands of Jesus followers participated in hundreds of local efforts to clean up schools, serve kids in foster care, and serve our refugee community. We celebrated this initial "season of service" with an outreach festival in our Waterfront Park that drew tens of thousands to eat great food, hear great music, and listen to a message of good news. That began an incredible journey lasting fourteen-plus years of collaboration among many, many churches.

Has it all been perfect? Absolutely not. We've made many mistakes. In particular, we didn't do a good enough job seeking to include non-English speaking churches and to include the wisdom and leadership of churches of color. The murder of George Floyd and the resulting one hundred-plus days of protesting that were unleashed in Portland revealed deep divisions within the community at large. And sadly, the church is not immune to these same divisions.

As is so often the case in the kingdom, out of the ashes, something beautiful was born. The rise in racial tension led to a fresh wave of humility and relationship building between majority-culture churches and churches of color. The leadership of the "movement" that began back in 2008 was reformed to be far more inclusive. A lot of listening and lamenting has taken place. That's led to a fresh vision for what we can do together to share Jesus, serve our schools, improve the lives of children in foster care, reduce gun violence, and in every way possible "seek the shalom" of the city where God has placed us.

Avery and I not only share a geographical "place" (Beaverton), we share a dream. If we could only see greater unity within the community of Jesus followers, we would rejoice more. We would understand God and ourselves more. We would see greater impact in the ways we love and serve and share the good news with so many that have rejected or neglected it.

Come join us on this adventure of faith, and be a part of fulfilling God's plan and Jesus' prayer, empowered by the Holy Spirit that lives within you.

KEVIN PALAU
President and CEO of the Luis Palau Association

Acknowledgments

To my wife, Nina, who supported me throughout this love assignment—Josh 24:15.

To my mom, Adella, who always exemplifies a mother's love—1 Sam 1:21–28.

To my children, Marlea, Stephan, and Kerrington, for whom I pray every day—Prov 4.

To my brothers Ruben Alvarado, Scott Dixon, Tom Greene, Frank Kane, and Dan McClure, who read every word and kept this project brewing—Prov 18:24.

To my doctoral mentor, Dr. Rick McKinley, who gave me his time, attention, and encouragement—Gal 6:9–10.

To my seminary dean, Dr. Derek Chinn, who graciously recommended me to Wipf & Stock—1 Cor 15:58.

To George Callihan and the team at Wipf & Stock, who said yes when others said no—Num 6:24–26.

And to my Common Ground Church family, who continues to amaze me by the way they love Christ, one another, and me—Phil 1:3-11.

Introduction

The opposite or lack of harmony.
It is used to describe a chord or interval where the notes clash.

—DISSONANCE (MUSIC THEORY)[1]

WE ARE LIVING IN an incredible time in human history when God's church can work together to bless the nations and, in the process, reset our narrative. Now is our time to be the church that looks like heaven.

But that is not where we are today.

It only took me nine minutes and twenty-nine seconds to see that the church is not one.

My adult children and all of their friends talked about that video for months. They were witnessing a global tipping point in real time.[2] The coronavirus pandemic forced dine-in restaurants to shift to takeout service only. Movies in theaters, concerts, and sporting events were all canceled. The presidential campaign was an ever-growing dumpster fire. Sheltering in place was a brand-new idea that was driving us crazy with cabin fever. Everyone was starving for entertainment and craving anything positive to take our minds off of our scary reality.

1. Epigraph quotes at the beginning of every chapter come from "Musical Dictionary."

2. The phrase "tipping point" is defined as "the moment of critical mass, the threshold, the boiling point." (Gladwell, *Tipping Point*, 12).

Then that video showed up on millions of mobile devices worldwide.

It was a horror show.

My daughter, two sons, and all of their friends watched a forty-six-year-old Black man publicly killed on the streets of Minneapolis while onlookers pressed record on their phones. Within minutes, podcasters rescheduled programming to talk about it. Outcries for racial justice sparked across the entire planet through the voices of college administrators, YouTubers, activists, celebrities, nonprofit moms' groups, prominent business owners, and so on. It was a worldwide phenomenon, the likes of which I had never seen in my lifetime. Protests ignited overnight like rabid wildfires through dry summer forest groves. Millions of everyday citizens took to their streets, chanting and screaming and insisting that Black lives mattered.

And how did the church respond?

One response was to speak in sync with the growing movement. Christians in urban, suburban, and rural settings used their voices to raise awareness of the cause. Many joined organized protests. Others adopted calls for racial reconciliation and justice, notably younger White churches and Christian leaders.[3] Still others posted book reading lists to encourage self-education on privilege, power, systemic racism, reparations, etc.

Soon after came a counterresponse from the church. As it turns out, the counterresponse was the loudest of all—a deafening silence from pulpits and pews across "America, my home sweet home." Those paralyzed voices never spoke those trending three words. Instead, when some decided to break their silence, they offered legal perspectives, biographical facts regarding the criminal

---

3. I will use the label "White" to correspond with the US Census Bureau's category of "White" race. I will also use the label "Black" to correspond with the US Census Bureau's category of "Black or African American" race. This is for the purpose of maintaining consistency throughout this book ("About Race"). Since "the Diversity Style Guide has long advocated for the capitalization of White as well as Black," I have elected to do the same (Kanigel, "White, White").

activities of victims, and an "all lives matter" chant to counter the escalating tidal wave.

I watched and waited.

One afternoon in late spring, I drove my oldest son to work when he asked, "Dad, are *you* gonna say something?" He is a profound thinker and often uses the confined space of my car to drop intellectual bombs on me. In that moment of hearing my son ask his pastor dad a pointed question, I felt the Holy Spirit tap me on the brain like Biff tapping George McFly on the noggin. I told him without blinking an eye, "Oh, yeah, Son. I *have* to."

I desperately wanted to point my son to the united "big-C Church" fully valuing his beautiful race, color, history, culture, and destiny. I wanted to show him a worldwide movement that was lifting up the name of Jesus by insisting that our Black lives matter too. I longed to redirect his attention to a united church with a gospel message that saves *souls* and saves *lives* from the devastating destruction of this world.

I still do . . .

But at that moment, the church's active and public division was crowding his media feeds.

The year 2020 was a societal and ecclesiastical pressure cooker; it was also the atmosphere under which I completed my doctoral thesis on local church collaboration. For eighteen months, while I researched and wrote how the body of Christ should come together to bless our world, I watched religious outsiders roll their eyes at our infighting and bickering. Friends and family reached out to me with screenshots of Christians virtually going at each other's throats. The more I wrote and preached and lamented, the more I saw our missed opportunities to make a splash for the gospel. If church leaders had taken our oneness in Christ more seriously, what could we have done together in the wake of this moment in time?

Before you dismiss this as subjective nonsense, let me fire off a short list of topics that Christians fought over in 2020 while my family and friends watched.

We publicly fought whether to use the word "murder" or "death" to describe the horror on that video. We debated the impact of Covid-19 and whether or not it was an actual global pandemic. Folks had knock-down-drag-out fights about whether or not to wear protective masks. We argued whether or not to obey government ordinances to suspend large public gatherings. Some church leaders said they followed God through civil disobedience, while others claimed godly obedience by submitting to civil authority. Then came the digital-vs.-analog church debate. Some congregations worshiped using digital platforms, while others insisted that worship was only acceptable to God when people gathered in person. Communion at home was another nasty argument. Some said it was permissible because Christ was the focus, while others claimed that self-serve communion invalidated the sacrament. If that were not enough, consider the ugliness that spewed out of our mouths during the Trump-Biden presidential election. Believers drew public lines in the sand, basing their tests of spiritual fellowship on the name cast on election ballots.

I am not saying that every believer must be a carbon copy of one another. I am also not saying that freedom in Christ prohibits nuances in theology, worldview, experiences, politics, opinions, or style. However, it is a big stinking problem if the predominant reputation of Christians is one of quarrelsome behavior and critical spirits. When we are known for who we dislike rather than for who we love, that is a problem.

But now . . .

A multitude of believers are anxious for something different.

Their timing could not be more perfect.

We are living in an incredible time in human history when God's church can work together to bless the nations and, in the process, reset our narrative. Now is our time to be the church that looks like heaven. And offering a biblical and practical way forward is the task of this project.

The rest of this work will reimagine local churches embracing collaboration as a normative practice of unity. Specifically, I will promote a culture of collaboration that mirrors the loving unity of the Trinity. Our discussion will reenvision what congregations can achieve together if their leaders highly value this kind of collaboration. Such a reimagined church would recast our reputation as the people who always work together in unity.

But let us not kid ourselves . . .

We will never get to collaboration if we cannot find our way to unity—even in disagreement!

So, this work also serves as a clarion call for Christian leaders to initiate new kingdom relationships, build new trust narratives, and leverage those narratives to pursue the gospel in their cities.

Every church will not be able to collaborate with *everyone*, but every church should collaborate with *someone*! And when your collaboration mirrors the Trinity, it is a work powered by the very definition of love—the Father, the Son, and the Holy Spirit. It helps us to fulfill Jesus' desire for his believers to be one. Yes, it only took me nine minutes and twenty-nine seconds to see that the church is not one. But it also only took one prayer from Jesus to convince me that we must be one!

If you decide to read on, you will encounter moments when the Holy Spirit will tap *you* on the noggin. Pay close attention to his stirrings. When it happens, you can either resist and excuse away why churches silo and remain strangers, or you can press into that moment. Remember, we have arrived where we are by doing what we have done. If you believe, like me, that Christ wants something different for his people, then stay with me while we talk about doing something different. I want him to do transformative work in your life like he continues to do in mine. After all, he is in the life-transformation business. Since collaboration is so important to me, it makes sense to begin this book by telling you why. So instead of leaving you in suspense, let us get to it.

A PRAYER

Father, I have need of you today. Refresh my mind and heart to find you and to see and know your will for me today. Be honored and glorified in all I see, do, think, and feel. Let me exalt your word, Jesus, above everything named. Come, Holy Spirit.

Carol Pilant
Ascension Church
Pittsburgh, Pennsylvania

Chapter 1

Mirrors

Where the primary beats of the music occur.

—Downbeat (music theory)

Local church collaboration is a beautiful practice of unity that mirrors the Trinity. The three persons of the Trinity proactively affirm and love one another in perfect harmony. No more extraordinary example exists and is worth pursuing or emulating. When collaboration builds on a foundation of authentic relationships, it can be an effective response to Jesus' prayer "that they may all be one, just as you, Father, are in me, and I in you" (John 17:21b).[1] Also, our displayed connection in Christ strengthens our credibility to share the gospel message. Jesus said, "By this, all people will know that you are my disciples if you have love for one another" (John 13:35). Church partnerships provide a chance to show a watchful world our love for one another, thereby identifying us as the followers of Christ. Outsiders are less likely to receive a message of hope from a divided church. Instead, our love—witnessed in kingdom partnership—can guide outsiders

---

1. Unless otherwise noted, Scripture texts are quoted from the English Standard Version (ESV) of the Bible.

from hostility toward God to transformation in Christ. No wonder Jesus called his followers "the light of the world. A city set on a hill cannot be hidden" (Matt 5:14). Believers must give outsiders access to see our patience, kindness, togetherness, and goodwill in action for them and one another. Local communities of faith that work together provide their neighbors and friends an inside look into the kingdom of God and direct access to the King of kings. Collaboration as a practice of unity deserves more significant consideration.

In support of this claim, this project will first address the gospel need for local church collaboration and why it should always mirror the loving unity of the Trinity.

AN HONEST LOOK IN THE MIRROR

Before writing my doctoral thesis, I had not given much thought to mirrors, let alone their place in literature and film lore. But my goodness, they are everywhere! Do you know the experience of buying a car that seemed unique, and then suddenly, after the purchase, you started seeing it on the road everywhere? That has been my comical experience lately with mirrors. Since my controlling thesis uses the imagery of a mirror, it might be fun to view a few ways that mirrors contribute to our lives. After all, mirrors have played pivotal casting roles in some of the greatest stories ever told.

A Whole Lotta Mirrors

For instance, the Brothers Grimm introduce us to an evil queen's morning conversations with an enchanted mirror in their nineteenth-century German fairy tale "Snow White." Walt Disney's adapted masterpiece depicts that evil queen on movie screens asking her enchanted costar, "Magic mirror on the wall, who's the fairest one of all?" The story plot dramatically turns when the mirror changes its affirming answer to (and this is my translation), "Sister, it ain't you!"

A memorable scene in *Harry Potter and the Sorcerer's Stone* is when young Harry longingly stares into the Mirror of Erised (the word "desire" spelled backward). Harry's wise professor warns his young, gifted student that the mirror is deceptive and alluring. "Dumbledore knows that life can pass you by while you are clinging on to a wish that can never be—or ought never to be—fulfilled."[2]

At least Harry eventually snaps out of it. According to Greek mythology, the hunter Narcissus died on the banks of "an untouched, glassy stream," mesmerized by his own mirrored reflection.[3]

"You talkin' to me?," the most famous line in all of Robert De Niro's movie career, would never have happened without his cinematic costar—a mirror.[4]

I discovered a gorgeous eighteenth-century Japanese fairy tale whose title transliterated from Japanese into English is *Matsuyama Kagami*. The title translated into English is *The Matsuyama Mirror*.[5] The brilliant writer pulls at his readers' heartstrings by penning a dying mother's final words as she tries to comfort her grieving young daughter.

> My darling child, you know that I am very sick: soon I must die and leave you and your dear father alone. When I am gone, promise me that you will look into this mirror every night and every morning: there you will see me and know that I am still watching over you." With these words, she took the mirror from its hiding place and gave it to her daughter. The child promised, with many tears, and so the mother, seeming now calm and resigned, died a short time after.[6]

This daughter has no idea that the mirror consistently produces "an image of whatever is in front of it."[7] So, the wise and

2. Rowling, "Mirror of Erised," para. 4.

3. Lin, "Narcissus Myth," para. 9.

4. "You Talkin' to Me?"

5. Hasegawa, *Matsuyama Mirror*.

6. Hasegawa, *Matsuyama Mirror*, 11–12.

7. *Cambridge Dictionary*, s.v. "mirror," https://dictionary.cambridge.org/

compassionate mother gives her daughter a gift more precious than the finest gems—a mirror that will always reflect her daughter's image, who looks ever so much like her mother. We all know the power that photographs wield to recall treasured memories of family and friends instantly. Similarly, the beloved mother empowers her daughter with the ability to visit her whenever she gazes into the mirror. This unique gift brings her comfort and joy.

Static and Dynamic Mirrors

Did you catch how mirrors can often function? On the one hand, they project static, emotionless representations of whatever is facing them. Discounting mirrors altered to maximize distortion, when you look into one, what you see is what you get. On the other hand, mirrors are notorious for offering a dynamic perspective for human beings. Even though they reflect static images, weird things happen once they land on our brains and hit our eyeballs. They evoke all kinds of responses, including (but not limited to) a sense of false security (the evil queen), bewilderment and wishful thinking (Harry Potter), delusions of grandeur (Narcissus), paranoia (Taxi Driver), or even peace, comfort, and joy (the girl from *The Matsuyama Mirror*).

We can get mad at the mirror because we dislike what we see. We can change the mirror in hopes of seeing something else. We can get rid of the mirror and look for a different one. We can question whether the mirror is working correctly. We can also face the fact that the mirror tells the truth, whether we like what we see or not. But if you decide to read on, I suggest you highlight or bookmark this page and these responses. Prepare yourself in advance to not be overwhelmed when excuses start flying around in your head.

---

us/dictionary/english/mirror.

ACTUALLY, THIS IS WHAT WE LOOK LIKE

If the body of Christ were able to stare into a mirror, what would she see reflected?

I contend that the church by design will resemble the Trinity's *unity among diversity*. Collaboration as a unity practice is a viable path for churches to live out Jesus' prayer in John 17. In other words, our metric for success comes directly from Jesus' own words: "That they may all be one, just as you, Father, are in me, and I in you" (John 17:21a). Humbly stepping in front of our allegorical mirror, we should always see God's oneness staring back at us.

Therein lies the angst of my thesis.

CHURCH GROWTH OR COLLABORATION

My experience is that the Church Growth Movement's metric of "greater resources, larger staffs, and intricate marketing campaigns among many other business-esque elements" is a more prevalent metric for success than *unity among diversity*.[8] In a manner of analogy, we looked into our kingdom mirror, saw the triune God's unity, and decided that we needed a different image to model. Even though John 17 was well and good, we gravitated toward Matt 28 and the Great Commission. Unity is the soft option that gets the golf handclap in our ecclesiastical vision and values. Making disciples and baptizing people—now that is where the real action lies. That is what makes our headlines, pays our bills, and motivates us to keep the Christian movement flowing.

Perhaps that is why church leaders stand in front of their mirrors with American-corporation aspirations as if to ask, Magic mirror on the wall, is my local church the fairest one of all?

Look at the evidence. Our churches have businesslike infrastructures resembling American corporations, including the lead pastors or ministers (CEO), elders and deacons (board of directors), members (shareholders), staff (executives), bylaws or vision/mission statements (articles of incorporation), ministry plans (business plans), and so on.[9] To say it bluntly, local churches prefer an image like businesses—selling similar products while competing for the same target customer base. And often, success is only

8. Stigile, "Would Jesus Want," para. 1.

9. See Reed, "Corporate Governance" for a description of how American corporations are run. I have drawn from Reed's description, applying it to the way churches are often run in the US.

felt when churches grab the lion's share of new customers in their given region (we call that evangelism or saving souls).

None of these things are wrong, and this project is not condemning these methods. But I maintain that we should view them as *methods* for ministry rather than *metrics* for church success.

Identify the markers of success in your church—which often center around Sunday attendance, money, programs, and property management. Consider the amount of time your leaders spend investing in their particular congregation's growth and stability (we call that stewardship). And more telling—consider what constitutes nonsuccess.

I spent many hours encouraging faithful pastors who felt like failures during the pandemic. The reality was that they cared for their congregations, served the people of their cities, and loved folks in their neighborhoods. And yet, they felt unsuccessful because of lower attendance for online gatherings, reduced financial revenue, canceled events, and so on. Why did they react this way, even while faithfully loving people? It is because our standard metrics for church success are different from the one promoted in this project—"that they may all be one" (John 17:21a).

PRESSURE TO GROW CHURCHES

I am honored to know church leaders, Christian communicators, and educators all over the United States and especially California and the Pacific Northwest. It is no exaggeration that I talked with hundreds of pastors while writing my thesis. Those who have confided in me on the subject of collaboration vs. church growth admitted feeling pressure to choose between building church partnerships and keeping their jobs. Their elder boards did not hire them to be kingdom ambassadors. Instead, they got hired to be successful staff employees for their congregations. So, when opportunities present themselves to partner with other believers in Jesus' name, these dedicated and passionate leaders find themselves saying no when they want to say yes. Unbeknownst to most church leaders, we syncretize the "Church Growth Movement"[10] principles with the gospel mission. Enmeshing both into twenty-first-century churches is part of the reason why pastors of smaller congregations feel unsuccessful even as faithful shepherds. We may not have read "Thou shalt build the biggest church possible to be pleasing to God" in the Bible, but we act as though it is in there somewhere. This ugly, debilitating stress conflicts with this project's theology of collaboration, which I will present in the next chapter. So, let us dive deeper and discuss a few pressure points.

The Pastor's Prime Directive: Grow the Church

Pastors and church leaders live under tremendous stress to lead growing churches, and this reality may be counterproductive in building the culture of local church collaboration. Job postings for available pastor positions fuel this pressure. One California church, for example, used the coded phrase "reaching our community" to communicate their growth expectations for their future hire. In another instance, a Colorado church skipped the coding altogether. Instead, they posted the following: "Position is Part-Time (16

---

10. C. Peter Wagner defines "church growth," as "all that is involved in bringing men and women who do not have a personal relationship to Jesus Christ into fellowship with Him and into responsible church membership" (Fong, *Wall*, 5–6). Wagner's major influence was Donald McGavran, dubbed the "father of church growth" and attributed with launching the Church Growth Movement in the 1970s (Stafford, "Father of Church Growth").

Hrs./Wk.) to Full Time (with growth of congregation)."[11] In other words, their future pastor's income will be contingent on his or her ability to produce increased attendance, baptisms, budget, ministry expansion, etc. As both examples indicate, church growth, their measure of success, defines their pastor's prime directives. To further understand this heaviness, let us look at how the Church Growth Movement defines itself.

People Movement or People Fencing?

Bruce Fong observed that "McGavran argued that the traditional 'Mission Station' approach to evangelism produced few results in comparison to the 'People Movement' approach. He further notes that 'more' is not depersonalizing but that each convert is a beloved person of God. Simply, ' . . . the more who come to Christian faith the better.'"[12] McGavran's emphasis on "people movement" as the best methodology for evangelism and the gospel was noble. Most church leaders I know aspire to belong to God's "people movement." But their jobs are to people fence, or people collect, or even people hoard. Such strategies result in churches that use growing numbers as the critical criteria of church success. This idea is core to the Church Growth Movement. The gospel can and has changed countless lives through the Church Growth Movement, but it has also enabled a culture of church isolation.

Sell, Sell, Sell

A friend of mine hired me in the mid-1980s to help him collect completed recruiting surveys for Westland College, a now-defunct vocational school. I was a young college student in need of cash, so I was motivated to do well. My friend got paid a particular dollar

---

11. Both of these job postings were found online on ChurchStaffing.com on April 20, 2020. I have chosen to maintain the anonymity of the hiring churches.

12. Fong, *Wall*, 6. Here, Fong quotes McGavran, *Bridges of God*, 97.

amount per completed survey, which is why he organized stacks of blank surveys on clipboards and had ink pens ready to go. He trained me to ask people to invest five minutes in answering a few questions that could change their lives. We stood for hours in front of grocery stores and unemployment offices on hot summer days, asking people to fill out surveys. I do not recall my friend's pay rate per survey, but there were weeks he received checks for over $1,000 for one week's work. He was quite an impressive salesman and was generous in paying me a percentage from all the surveys I collected.

The tension did not stop there. We were promoting Westland College while I was attending Fresno State. We pointed folks looking for new careers or new skills toward Westland, even though we were not the actual college recruiters. After we collected the completed forms, my friend handed them to the recruiting office so that the salaried recruiters could contact the prospects. I remember feeling like I was endorsing a product that I had never tried. To use an old commercial as an analogy, I sold HairClub for Men, but I was not a client.

Therein lies my felt pressure—get people to fill out surveys or do not get paid.

Services Rendered

Similar pressure to sell, sell, sell is the inner stress that gospel ministers feel from their leaders. The model we used comes from the mirrored image we prefer to see—payment for services rendered. Here is another revealed secret. Pastors often feel a dichotomy between their calling and their jobs. They are clients to the gospel mission; that is what they signed up to do for the rest of their lives. After getting the church gig, they discovered that their jobs were secure as long as they made their congregations happy. Perhaps you see now why I used the word "stress." Let me repeat my statement: pastors and church leaders live under tremendous stress to lead growing churches, and this reality may be counterproductive in building the culture of local church collaboration.

I invite church leaders to reimagine how pastoral work would appear if their governance modeled how the Father, Son, and Holy Spirit relate to one another. This reimagined work is the same task as how we are reframing kingdom partnerships.

Competition

When numerical growth is the measure of church success, one common by-product is a spirit of competition among local church pastors. To get as many people as possible into our church doors, we plan "bring a friend" days, "back to school" events, fall kickoffs, Vacation Bible Clubs, special CME worship gatherings (Christmas, Mother's Day, and Easter), etc. We send mass postcard mailings, purchase printed materials from Christian marketing firms, download visual backgrounds for sermon slides that match the printed materials, and on and on. These things are well-intentioned methods to spread the gospel in our cities. But honestly, does your city need one hundred Vacation Bible Clubs in a ten-mile radius? My guess is no.

Let me expose another great secret to all of you. The best resource for your church's gospel success is not a Christian marketing firm to help you pull off spectacular events. Your church's best resource for a compelling gospel mission lies within the hearts and lives of people who attend other churches in your city. They are committed to their congregations, and rightfully so. They are faithfully serving in a community of faith that blesses them with authentic friendships and spiritual training. They are not prospects for your church, and they probably never will be. Yet, by design, they are the finest resource available to you for gospel impact. They can help you convince the world that Jesus Christ is the light of the world. You *need* one another, and it is high time that you met!

Job Insecurity

Churches do not usually hire pastors to collaborate with other churches. That job objective would seemingly conflict with building the membership and financial stability of the hiring church. Collaboration would be outside the boundaries of pastoral ministry. No wonder pastors feel unmotivated to build kingdom partnerships—the work of practicing unity among believers is not their job. Doing anything "on the clock" that is not part of their job contracts can be grounds for dismissal. That is real pressure.

COLLABORATION CAN REDEFINE SUCCESS

A benefit that collaboration brings to the ideology of church growth is that success becomes measured by the achievements of every partnered church. Any soul that comes to Jesus through your church partnerships is one for all to celebrate and rejoice. Every family battling the loss of a child becomes a family for all of us to cover in prayer. In these examples, one congregation is the primary community of faith while the others come alongside to bless and encourage them as the church of Jesus Christ. This kind of collaboration believes that when one grows, we all grow; when one is lost, we all feel the loss. When one congregation wins, we all win. We become active participants in the oneness of the Trinity.

2020 KILLED OUR METRICS FOR SUCCESS

The global pandemic shook our emotions and crushed our plans. Once government officials issued stay-at-home orders across the nation, every contributing factor in the Church Growth Movement model was either drastically limited or eliminated. Ministry calendars became irrelevant overnight. Printed bulletins and attendance cards were suddenly a waste of money and ink. Welcome teams, Sunday set-up crews, parking-lot attendants, campus-security teams, guest-services teams, children-ministry workers, communion set-up teams, and so on lost their primary outlet to serve people. With less than a week's notice, every church that I am familiar with saw every contributing factor to the church-growth model fly out the window. Pastors who were previously *successful* in their church-growth strategies got their worlds rocked. I know of church leaders who quit, got fired, experienced panic attacks, developed high blood pressure, and even died from stress-exacerbated illnesses.

My friend Chris Gough told me an analogy that beautifully described our dilemma. If the church was a chess game, Sunday mornings were the queen—the one piece on the board that could do it all—and God snatched the queen off the board and said, "Now let's see if you can still play the game." Many churches shook with fear during the pandemic and lost their way. Because Sunday gatherings are one-stop vending machines for all things spiritual, and the pandemic unplugged the vending machine and spoiled all of the items, we were left unprepared to know if we were still able to be God's church. How would we lead worship, make announcements, receive financial offerings, spiritually train new believers, and so on? Our preferred image of being a successful American corporation in 2020 showed us how unsuccessful, technologically deficient, and fiscally unstable we were. We compared ourselves against that model, and we did not measure up. And I am screaming at the top of my lungs, *We are mirroring the wrong thing!*

Hear the heart of the Son of God again as he looked into our future: "That they may all be one, just as you, Father, are in me, and I in you, that they also may be in us" (John 17:21). Christ knew that we would try to accomplish his mission on our own and mess it all up. In his high priestly prayer, he provided the only perfect image for his people to mirror. So, let us consider our mirror. Keep reading, and we will discuss God's uniqueness and harmonious community—this project's local-church-collaboration metrics.

DEVOTIONAL REFLECTIONS
(INDIVIDUALLY OR IN SMALL GROUPS)

1. Finish these two statements:

   "I use mirrors to . . ."

   "My home church reminds me of a . . ." (analogy like family, business, hospital, social club, etc.). Would you please explain your responses (in small groups, share your explanations)?

2. Read John 17 in its entirety. Use your favorite translation plus a paraphrase like Eugene Peterson's The Message. Which verses (or words) in Jesus' prayer draw your attention? Spend five minutes highlighting them in your Bible or writing them down.

3. What are the indicators that a church is a) mirroring the relational oneness of the Father and the Son, or b) using a different mirror to measure church growth? Write your responses down (in small groups, compare lists).

4. From the previous question, in which indicators from the "first mirror" are you and your church excelling? In need of movement? What about the "second" mirror? Write your responses down (in small groups, compare lists).

5. Prayer focus: "God, help my church-growth indicators to reflect the heart of Christ."

6. Song of reflection: "Don't Pass Me By" as performed by TONE6.

A PRAYER

Father,

Change our stubborn hearts into your likeness through the Spirit's conviction and discipline.

Remembering that you are the God who sees (Gen 16:13 NIV), may we daily be reminded that what our Father desires is what his children should also desire—let us be a people who see. The way you see others.

Remind us that you first loved us. Not the other way around. And manifested that love in holy flesh that was offered for us. And because of this, please accept our offering of ourselves and forgive our idolatries, as we embrace with humility our commission of loving humanity—like you do—everywhere and in any fashion. Even where there is discomfort, rejection, and peril.

Let us accept the Spirit's work in us, and accept the work you have called us into—unity work.

As you are one, make us one in you.

In Jesus the Messiah, amen.

Bruce Williams
Northwest Church
Lynnwood, Washington

Chapter 2

The God Who Wants to Be Known

Instruments/different voices playing the same pitches together.

—Unison (musical term)

GOD SOUNDS LIKE DARTH VADER?

Ask a child, "What does God look like?" then sit back and take notes. I performed a Google search on this subject and found some thought-provoking drawings from kids depicting the Almighty. Some characteristics were pretty unanimous. He is almost always White and old, smiles all the time, has a thick and long beard, lives in the sky surrounded by clouds, and usually has people and animals nearby. I remember as a child seeing Jesus' portrait on printed hand fans that advertised the local funeral home. He was a thin-faced White man with long curly hair and blue eyes. You could tell by looking at him that he cared for people but could benefit from a good meal of a burger and fries. The other side of the fan had two popular options. Black funeral homes had Dr. King opposite Jesus, and White funeral homes had John F. Kennedy opposite Jesus.

Our church sang a hymn called "Watching You."

All along on the road to the soul's true abode,

There's an eye watching you;

Ev'ry step that you take this great eye is awake,

There's an eye watching you.

Watching you, watching you,

Ev'ry day mind the course you pursue,

Watching you, watching you,

There's an all-seeing eye watching you.[1]

Those words did not evoke an invitation for intimacy with God. Instead, in my childlike mind, they conjured the image of a great giant eyeball in the sky, waiting for me to mess up so that God could zap me with lightning bolts.

Maybe God looks like Mufasa, the mighty lion who rules over the Pride Lands and sounds precisely like Darth Vader. Perhaps he seems more like Q the Omnipotent, giving Captain Picard and his crew fits on *Star Trek: The Next Generation*. Maybe you view God as a terrifying bald head sitting bodiless on a throne in the middle of a large room and daring you to speak. How disappointing it would be to discover that God was an ordinary man manipulating you behind a curtain.

GOD WANTS TO BE KNOWN

Perhaps it is just me (though I doubt it), but God can be a little intimidating to comprehend. Yet, the Scriptures reveal that God wants to be known. He wants people to recognize his image readily. He desires a heart-to-heart connection with humanity.

From the Psalms: "Be still, and know that I am God" (Ps 46:10). From Paul's letter to the Roman church: "For his invisible attributes, namely, his eternal power and divine nature, have been

1. Henson, "Watching You."

clearly perceived, ever since the creation of the world, in the things that have been made. So they are without excuse" (Rom 1:20). Addressing the Epicurean and Stoic philosophers on Mars Hill about "the God who made the world and everything in it, being Lord of heaven and earth," Paul told them, "that they should seek God, and perhaps feel their way toward him and find him. Yet he is actually not far from each one of us" (Acts 17: 24, 27). This triune God wants men and women, boys and girls, to find him. I take comfort in knowing this humbling truth.

Over the years, I have asked the Holy Spirit to grant me more insight into who he is and why he loves me so intimately despite my brokenness and failings. Therefore, I offer this personal note in hopes that you will take comfort in seeking the true God. He desires to know you, and he invites you to know him.

But I need to be specific about who God is. I am referring to the God of the Bible. His voice is much more majestic than the voice of James Earl Jones!

AFFIRMING THE TRINITY

The doctrine of the one true God—Father, Son, and Holy Spirit— is fundamental to Christian orthodoxy. This central reality differentiates Christianity from other world faiths. Karl Barth penned, "The doctrine of the Trinity is what basically distinguishes the Christian doctrine of God as Christian, and therefore what already distinguishes the Christian concept of revelation as Christian, in contrast to all other possible doctrines of God or concepts of revelation."[2]

The Council of Nicea in 325 was a collaborative effort to halt the heretical teachings of an Alexandrian priest named Arius. He taught that "if God was unknowable, then Jesus could not be God in the same sense that the Father is because Jesus is knowable. Further, if God is both one and indivisible, then clearly Jesus must be both other than and after God—a kind of higher divine creature,

2. Barth, *Church Dogmatics*, 301.

but not one with and sharing in the divine nature of the Father."[3] Arius' chief opponent was a fellow Alexandrian named Athanasius. His effort to establish Trinitarianism as orthodoxy spurred the council to convene on the matter. In their final confession, known as the Nicene Creed, the term *homoousios* spoke specifically to the divine nature of Jesus Christ: "With this word, the church declared that the second person of the Trinity has the same substance or essence as the Father, thereby affirming that the Father, the Son, and the Holy Spirit are equal in being and eternality."[4]

Robert Letham also affirms the Trinity with the following five descriptions of God, saying that the Trinity is: (1) "one being—three persons; three persons—one being," (2) "three *homoousios* persons," (3) "three persons mutually indwelling one another in a dynamic communion," (4) "three persons irreducibly different from one another," and (5) "three who have an order (taxis) among the persons."[5]

The beauty of our God is that there is clarity within his complexity. There is intimacy within his awesomeness. There is community innate to his nature. I join these theologians, writers, and great thinkers in affirming the one true God, who is Father, Son, and Holy Spirit. I also confess that my journey to know him fully is far from complete.

WHY MIRROR THE TRINITY?

It is one thing to affirm the doctrine of the Trinity; it is another thing to assert that local church collaboration should mirror the Trinity. Let me offer two theological reasons. First, since God is one in his uniqueness, the "big-C Church"[6] should be one. Sec-

---

3. "Arius and Nicea," para. 3.

4. Sproul, "Athanasian Creed," para. 1.

5. Letham, *Holy Trinity*, 202.

6. The term "big-C Church" refers to the one church that Jesus built. I use it to emphasize our spiritual connection to the worldwide network of assembled believers.

ond, since God is inherently a relational community, the big "C" Church should be too.

When the body of believers exhibits these characteristics, the church reflects the triune nature of her God. It is crucial, then, that local congregations intentionally foster both this unity and kindred connection with one another to better reflect her God to a watching world.

FIRST REASON: GOD IS ONE IN HIS UNIQUENESS

There is only one God who exists in three persons. More than that, the triune God is one because he is unique. The Holy Scriptures are full of rich doctrines affirming the uniqueness of God. This examination will start with a foundational tenet of the Hebrew faith—the Shema.

The Shema

The Shema, referring "to a couple lines from the book of Deuteronomy (6:4–5),"[7] begins "Hear, O Israel: The Lord our God, the Lord is one" (Deut 6:4). According to Tim Mackie, the Shema was the foundational doctrine that became an ancient traditional Israelite prayer. His translation from the Hebrew text to English reads, "Listen, Israel, the Lord is our God, the Lord alone."[8] Noting the translation concerns of where to place the English verb *is* in the phrase "*YHWH 'elohenu YHWH ekhad*," Mackie contends that the danger of polytheism along the Israelites' journey to Canaan justifies a translation favoring a theology of the uniqueness of God. YHWH is the God of the Israelites and the only God.[9] No wonder that when a scribe asked Jesus to identify the greatest commandment, he answered, "The most important is, 'Hear, O Israel: The Lord our God, the Lord is one. And you shall love the Lord your

7. Mackie, "What is the Shema?," para. 1.
8. Mackie, "What is the Shema?," para. 1
9. Mackie, "What is the Shema?," para. 9.

God with all your heart and with all your soul and with all your mind and with all your strength'" (Mark 12:29–30). No wonder Paul could leverage the Athenians' altar "to the unknown god" as an opportunity to preach about the only God: "The God who made the world and everything in it, being Lord of heaven and earth, does not live in temples made by man, nor is he served by human hands, as though he needed anything, since he himself gives to all mankind life and breath and everything" (Acts 17:24–25). Thus, it seems appropriate for me to build a trinitarian theology of collaboration at the same starting point of the Israelites' theology of God—"Hear, O Israel: The Lord our God, the Lord is one" (Deut 6:4).

There is No One Like God

The Hebrew scriptures testify that there is no one like God. Moses wanted Pharaoh to know that the plague of frogs would only cease at the command of the one true God. "Be it as you say, so that you may know that there is no one like the Lord our God" (Exod 8:10). He pleaded with God for entrance into the promised land. "O Lord God, you have only begun to show your servant your greatness and your mighty hand. For what god is there in heaven or on earth who can do such works and mighty acts as yours?" (Deut 3:24). King David expressed thanks even though God denied him the honor of building the temple. "Therefore, you are great, O Lord God. For there is none like you, and there is no God besides you, according to all that we have heard with our ears" (2 Sam 7:22). In Jeremiah's praise discourse of the foolishness of gods made of wood and earthly stones, he said, "But the Lord is the true God; he is the living God and the everlasting King. At his wrath, the earth quakes, and the nations cannot endure his indignation. Thus shall you say to them: 'The gods who did not make the heavens and the earth shall perish from the earth and from under the heavens'" (Jer 10:10–11). Moses, David, and Jeremiah believed that God possessed true power to create and rule the universe. But he is much more than these things. He is the God that is uniquely Father.

Uniquely Father, Not Just Creator or Ruler

Michael Reeves wrote about the uniqueness of God as Father, not just Creator or Ruler. First, "if God's very identity is to be The Creator, The Ruler, then he needs a creation to rule to be who he is. For all his cosmic power, then, this God turns out to be pitifully weak: he needs us."[10] Secondly, if we identify him primarily as a ruler, our salvation is solely dependent on keeping the rules.[11] The only viable answer to these problems is to identify him through Jesus Christ as Father: "The God [that Jesus] reveals is, first and foremost, a Father. 'I am the way and the truth and the life,' he says. 'No one comes to the Father except through me' (John 14:6). That is who God has revealed himself to be: not first and foremost Creator or Ruler, but Father." [12]

Furthermore, Reeves says, "He creates as a Father, and he rules as a Father, and that means the way he rules over creation is most unlike the way any other God would rule over creation."[13] This quote speaks to the true uniqueness of God. He has always been Father, and Jesus is the proof of that. "The Father is the lover; the Son is the beloved."[14] The Spirit is the affirmation of the Father's love for his son. "It is, then, through giving him the Spirit that the Father declares his love for the Son."[15] Fred Sanders reminds us why God is the Father: "He would have been God the Father if he had never adopted created sons and daughters because he would have been God the Father of God the Son."[16] This truth that God is Father, not just Creator or Ruler, shows the Trinity to be one of a kind indeed. But how so is the Trinity—meaning Father, Son, and Holy Spirit—unique?

---

10. Reeves, *Delighting in the Trinity*, 19.

11. Reeves, *Delighting in the Trinity*, 20.

12. Reeves, *Delighting in the Trinity*, 21.

13. Reeves, *Delighting in the Trinity*, 23.

14. Reeves, *Delighting in the Trinity*, 28.

15. Reeves, *Delighting in the Trinity*, 29.

16. Sanders, *Deep Things of God*, 92.

Unique in His Invitation to Humanity

When asked how the Trinity is unique, I cannot conceive a more excellent answer than God's invitation for humanity to unite with him in family relationships. Two remarkable scriptures encapsulate this invitation.

First, "For God so loved the world, that he gave his only Son, that whoever believes in him should not perish but have eternal life" (John 3:16–17). Through the Son's sacrifice on Calvary, God invites humanity to live eternally with him. This invitation is extraordinary and hard to conceive.

The second aspect of his invitation is equally remarkable: "God made him who had no sin to be sin for us so that in him we might become the righteousness of God" (2 Cor 5:21 NIV). Humans could never accept God's generous invitation of eternal life because of our sin—"for all have sinned and fall short of the glory of God" (Rom 3:23). Likewise, we could never accept his invitation because of God's wrath against sin. "For the wrath of God is revealed from heaven against all ungodliness and unrighteousness of men, who by their unrighteousness suppress the truth" (Rom 1:18). As Moses could attest, our humanness is so flawed that we could never look upon God's face and survive the experience (Exod 33:17–23). Yet, this unique triune God invites us (because of the work of Christ) to "become the righteousness of God," thereby covering our sin with Christ's blood, satisfying his dreadful wrath and positioning us to receive his invitation of eternal life. His love is so unique that he is "not wishing that any should perish, but that all should reach repentance" (2 Pet 3:9). I am unaware of any claim to deity in any other religion that involved that same deity's sacrificial death for the sake of humanity's path to enter his eternal family. This remarkable truth is why Paul was confident to speak to the Athenian philosophers of this unique God. "And [God] made from one man every nation of mankind to live on all the face of the earth, having determined allotted periods and the boundaries of their dwelling place, that they should seek God, and perhaps feel their way toward him and find him" (Acts 17:26–27a). He invites us and wants us to find him! The Father's willingness to sacrifice his Son so that we can become his righteousness and enter into his eternal life is how this God is uniquely one of a kind.

On the heels of his redemptive sacrifice, Jesus took time to pray. Think about this:

Minutes before walking to Gethsemane—

Betrayal and Roman nails encumbering his every step—

The Son of God made *us* a key point in his high priestly prayer to his Father.

He intentionally underscored God's desire for his believers— "that they may be one *as we are one.*"

His desire ought to be *ours*.

APPLICATION: THE CHURCH SHOULD BE ONE AS GOD IS ONE

Collaboration is a practical way for churches to exercise and model our unique calling and unity in Christ. I suggest that unity must be a lived-out reality, not just a theological construct. Collaboration can provide a method to live out the truth of our oneness in Christ. It visually reminds us that Christ designed his followers to be one, just like the Trinity. In practice, we will then reflect his glory—we mirror him.

Only One Church

Jesus built only one church. "And I tell you, you are Peter, and on this rock, I will build my church, and the gates of hell shall not prevail against it" (Matt 16:18). Jesus used a word familiar to the Jews to describe a brand-new idea called 'the church.' The Greek word ἐκκλησία (pronounced ek-kla-se'-ä) referred to "an assembly of the people convened at the public place of the council for the purpose of deliberating."[17] Jesus purposely used the singular

---

17. *Strong's Lexicon*, s.v. "*ekklēsia*," https://www.blueletterbible.org/lexicon/g1577/esv/mgnt/0-1/.

form of ἐκκλησία and not the plural form ἐκκλησίαις as John did when addressing his letter "to the seven churches that are in Asia" (Rev 1:4). He intended to build one divine assembly of people (ἐκκλησία).

Along with his initial disciples, this church of Jesus Christ would represent him on earth. That is why Paul calls the Corinthian believers "ambassadors for Christ" (2 Cor 5:20). Furthermore, the New Testament refers to the church as the singular body of Christ: "There is one body and one Spirit—just as you were called to the one hope that belongs to your call" (Eph 4:4). Since there is only one body, there is only one church. The New Testament also speaks of Christ as head of that body, bringing its diverse members into unity and oneness. "For the husband is the head of the wife even as Christ is the head of the church, his body, and is himself its Savior" (Eph 5:23). Thus, every soul around the world assembled in Jesus' name collectively form the one (and only) ἐκκλησία of Jesus Christ.

Intentional Unity among Many Congregations

Paul taught the Corinthians that "because there is one bread, we who are many are one body, for we all partake of the one bread" (1 Cor 1:17). And likewise, to the Galatians: "There is neither Jew nor Greek, there is neither slave nor free man, there is neither male nor female; for you are all one in Christ Jesus" (Gal 3:28). This apostle believed that Jesus followers spiritually link together through Christ. He is our common ground.

And yet, Jesus knew that his one (and only) church would need to be intentional in their unity, connection, and oneness. Listen to his heart's desire:

> I do not ask for these only, but also for those who will believe in me through their word, that they may all be one, just as you, Father, are in me, and I in you, that they also may be in us, so that the world may believe that you have sent me. (John 17:20–21)

It is my experience that churches with established cultures that practice unity with other local churches are rare. Most churches embrace the idea of unity but struggle to know a realized vision of unity. What is now rare must become a flourishing orchard rooted in God's call to be one. Collaborating churches must become the rule rather than the exception.

Let me give you two reasons why from John 17.

First, our practiced unity is proof of our connection to God.

Look again at how Jesus links our oneness to his own: "Just as you, Father, are in me, and I in you, that *they also may be in us*" (John 17:21b, emphasis mine). To paraphrase, "Father, help my followers collaborate now so that they can eternally experience the real thing in us!"

Second, Jesus tethers our oneness to the world's faith in Christ.

Believers must intentionally be one "so that the world *may believe that you have sent me*" (John 17:21c, emphasis mine). What strong language from the Savior. Our displayed collaboration provides the world with a visible affirmation of the incarnation. In other words, Jesus knew that "our witness to the world hinges on our unity."[18] These reasons strengthen my resolve to see Jesus' prayer realized in our generation.

No excuses are ever valid enough to dismiss Christ's intent for his body. Therefore, any laissez-faire approaches to collaboration seem off-script for anyone desiring to be God's earthly community. Since nothing has the power "to separate us from the love of God in Christ Jesus our Lord" (Rom 8:39), we must never allow *anything* to prevent us from active partnerships with other churches in our city. This project strongly encourages leaders to be more intentional with their expressions of unity among many congregations.

18. Greer et al., *Rooting for Rivals*, 31.

SECOND REASON: GOD IS AN INDIVISIBLY UNITED COMMUNITY

In addition to being one in uniqueness, the three-in-one God is always indivisibly united in everything the persons of the Trinity do.

First and Foremost Relational

The Godhead's united community rises from the eternal truth that the Trinity is first and foremost relational. Sanders discusses this truth in chapter 3 of *The Deep Things of God*. In summary, to be God means to be Father, Son, and Holy Spirit. He has always been content to love and communicate and affirm himself eternally. God never created out of a need to be productive. He is God and has always been God, which is Sanders's critical point in the chapter. "It would be wrong to say that God created because he was lonely, unfulfilled, or bored. . . . The perfect blessedness of God would not have been compromised by the final failure of humanity. God did not save us to rescue himself from sadness over our plight. He saved us freely, out of an astonishing abundance of generosity."[19]

Darrell Johnson underscores the relational nature of the Trinity:

> "At the center of the universe is a relationship." That is the most fundamental truth I know. At the center of the universe is a community. It is out of that relationship that you and I were created and redeemed. And it is for that relationship that you and I were created and redeemed! And it turns out that there is a three-fold-ness to that relationship. It turns out that the community is a Trinity. The center of reality is Father, Son, and Holy Spirit.[20]

God's relational community is why kingdom partnerships should always launch from a foundation of relationships. In this way, collaboration mirrors the triune God, who is first and foremost relational.

19. Sanders, *Deep Things of God*, 71.
20. Johnson, *Experiencing the Trinity*, 37.

In Creation

I observe an intentional practice of unity in the creation of human life: "Then God said, 'Let us make man in our image, after our likeness'" (Gen 1:26a). The genesis of humanity is a beautiful picture of the one and only God of heaven: the Father, Son, and Holy Spirit displaying their united oneness.

At Jesus' Baptism

Matthew shows their unity in action: "And when Jesus was baptized, immediately he went up from the water, and behold, the heavens were opened to him, and he saw the Spirit of God descending like a dove and coming to rest on him; and behold, a voice from heaven said, 'This is my beloved Son, with whom I am well pleased'" (Matt 3:16–17). This text highlights their mutually self-giving community. The Father affirmed the Son as his anointed, and the Holy Spirit confirmed the Father's testimony.

In Isaiah's Messianic Prophecy

Isaiah refers to the Messiah, the Son, as God: "For to us a child is born, to us, a son is given; and the government shall be upon his shoulder, and his name shall be called Wonderful Counselor, Mighty God, Everlasting Father, Prince of Peace" (Isa 9:6). The Son, distinct from God the Father and God the Spirit, is entirely "Mighty God." Paul confirms this with the new believers in Colossae: "For in [Christ] all the fullness of God was pleased to dwell, and through him to reconcile to himself all things, whether on earth or in heaven, making peace by the blood of his cross" (Col 1:19). Every bit of God's fullness lives and thrives within Jesus. The Son is indivisibly united with the Father and the Spirit.

At Mary's Visitation

All three persons of the Trinity appear in Mary's conversation with an angel: "And the angel answered her, 'The Holy Spirit will come upon you, and the power of the Most High will overshadow you; therefore the child to be born will be called holy—the Son of God'" (Luke 1:35). In this text, the Spirit, the Most High (the Father), and the Son work together in perfect unity for the Messiah's birth.

At the Great Commission

This triunity appears in the Great Commission: "Go therefore and make disciples of all nations, baptizing them in the name of the Father and of the Son and of the Holy Spirit" (Matt 28:19). This same triunity appears in the apostle Paul's benediction in 2 Corinthians: "The grace of the Lord Jesus Christ and the love of God and the fellowship of the Holy Spirit be with you all" (2 Cor 13:14). These are a sampling of scriptures showing the inseparable unity of the Father, Son, and Holy Spirit. Together, as stated in the Nicene Creed, they are the three-in-one and one-in-three Trinity.[21]

Diversity within Supreme Harmony

It is vital to briefly consider the intentional diversity within the Trinity's threeness because it ties directly to this project's thesis.

The one true God is wonderfully diverse and distinct as Father, Son, and Holy Spirit in supreme harmony.[22] Johnson says that the doctrine of the Trinity preserves three truths: 1) "there is one God and only one God," 2) "this God not only exists, but exists (and subsists) eternally in three distinct persons," and 3) "the three persons are equally divine in essence and attributes."[23]

---

21. Reardon, "Nicene and Apostles' Creeds."

22. I am borrowing the coined phrase "supreme harmony" from Jonathan Edwards (see Pauw, *Supreme Harmony*).

23. Johnson, *Experiencing the Trinity*, 41.

Reeves's description of this oneness and why it makes a difference that we have a three-person God is also helpful:

> *Oneness* for the single-person God would mean *sameness*. Alone for eternity without any beside him, why would he value others and their differences? Think how it works out for Allah: under his influence, the once-diverse cultures of Nigeria, Persia, and Indonesia are made, deliberately and increasingly, *the same*. Islam presents a complete way of life for individuals, nations, and cultures, binding them into one way of praying, one way of marrying, buying, fighting, relating—even, some would say, one way of eating and dressing.
>
> *Oneness* for the triune God means *unity*. As the Father is absolutely one with his Son, and yet is not his Son, so Jesus prays that believers might be one, but not that they might all be the same. Created male *and* female, in the image of this God, and with many other good differences between us, we come together valuing the way the triune God has made us each unique.[24]

Rowan Williams provides additional help with his understanding of St. Augustine's views about Christ and the Trinity: "The Father is distinct from the Son because he stands in the relation of a source to what flows from it; the Son relates to the Father as a life or agency that is derived, not simply generative; Father and Son relate to Spirit as giving agencies relate to gift. In Father, Son, and Spirit, one identical life is lived; but it is lived as generating, as generated, as given. Only in these modes is it real."[25]

The diversity within the Trinity communicates why and how his people are such a "great multitude that no one could number, from every nation, from all tribes and peoples and languages" (Rev 7:9). His nature models creative variety from the center of the universe. This point is not a small one. Our diversity in the family of God is a spiritual coalition of unique image bearers linked together by Christ. As such, individuals never have to decolorize or dampen their brilliance while in the body. On the contrary,

24. Reeves, *Delighting in the Trinity*, 103–4.
25. Williams, *On Augustine*, 137.

our collective diversity is a beautiful reflection of God's diversity. Churches would do well to include diverse voices in their gospel planning. When we actively and visibly celebrate our diversity, we mirror the Trinity.

APPLICATION: THE CHURCH SHOULD BE AN INDIVISIBLY UNITED COMMUNITY

God's church is being built, by the Holy Spirit, into the fullness of Christ the Son, who is the exact image of the Father. The triune God is therefore transforming the church *into his image*. Did you catch that analogy for the church? Our aim ought to be mirroring the self-giving community of the Trinity. Local congregations reflect their unity when they operate together as the one body of Christ.

While distinct, the Father, Son, and Holy Spirit never silo, live independently, or function as disconnected entities. That would be polytheism. Congregations must reflect those same attributes by the way they partner in the gospel mission. I will further elaborate when we review this project's model for collaboration.

Local Congregations in the New Testament

The New Testament introduces us to many churches: Jerusalem, Rome, Ephesus, Philippi, all over Galatia, Colossae, Thessalonica, Laodicea, Philadelphia, Thyatira, Smyrna, Pergamum, Sardis, and others. All of them had a connection with one another through the blood of Jesus Christ. All of them together made up the New Testament ecosystem of the one church.

Regarding the community of believers, Paul wrote to the church in Ephesus, "There is one body and one Spirit—just as you were called to the one hope that belongs to your call—one Lord, one faith, one baptism, one God and Father of all, who is over all and through all and in all" (Eph 4:4–6). Likewise, to the church in Corinth, he wrote, "For just as the body is one and has many members, and all the members of the body, though many, are one body, so it is with Christ" (1 Cor 12:12).

In his communication with the Corinthians, Paul warned against disunity: "I appeal to you, brothers, by the name of our Lord Jesus Christ, that all of you agree, and that there be no divisions among you, but that you be united in the same mind and the same judgment" (1 Cor 1:10). He told the Ephesian church to be "eager to maintain the unity of the Spirit in the bond of peace" (Eph 4:3).

When the apostle to the Gentiles needed to write to several congregations of believers, he addressed them as "the churches of Galatia" (Gal 1:2). He said, "For in Christ Jesus, you are all sons of God, through faith. For as many of you as were baptized into Christ have put on Christ. There is neither Jew nor Greek; there is neither slave nor free, there is no male and female, for you are all one in Christ Jesus" (Gal 3:26–28).

When churches begin seeing themselves as congregations of the one church, they will start fulfilling their designed purpose as an indivisibly united community of believers in Jesus Christ (John 17:20–21).

SUMMARY OF WHY OUR COLLABORATION SHOULD MIRROR THE TRINITY

I built my answer on two theological reasons.

First, God is uniquely one, so *the church should mirror him by being uniquely one.*

His loving oneness is our design, so we must emulate him. This project promotes collaboration as a way for the church to live into her uniqueness in Christ.

Second, God is triune: three distinct persons in an inseparable community of the Father, Son, and Holy Spirit. Therefore, *the church should mirror him by being an indivisibly united community.*

Though a bit odd sounding, God himself ought to be the church's measure for practicing loving unity through collaboration.

IS THIS EVEN ACHIEVABLE?

We have established why the church should collaborate to mirror the Trinity, but that begs a brutally honest question: "Is this even achievable? Seriously, can I *get real* for a minute?" Both questions are legit!

So, let us get real for a minute.

The Gift of His Glory

The Son of God believes we can be one, so I do too. He gave us his glory so that we could achieve it.

"Glory" in John 17 is the English translation of the Greek word δόξαν (dóxan), a form of δόξα (dox'-ah). Its usage means "a good opinion concerning one (or renown), resulting in praise, honor."[26] Jesus shared glory with the Father "before the world existed" (John 17:5). That same glory was his gift to us.

> "The glory that you have given me I have given to them, that they may be one even as we are one, I in them and you in me, that they may become perfectly one" (John 17:22-23a).

Did you catch that incredible provision? He extended his praiseworthy reputation to his believers so that we may be one. This same renown was relished by the psalmist: "The heavens declare the glory of God, and the sky above proclaims his handiwork" (Ps 19:1).

But wait, there's more—

His glory has resurrection power. Jesus told Martha moments before raising Lazarus from the dead, "Did I not tell you that if you believed you would see the glory of God" (John 11:40)? His magnificent glory has the power to command life and death; it is also a provision powerful enough to bind us together in perfect oneness.

---

26. *Strong's Lexicon*, s.v. "*doxa*," https://www.blueletterbible.org/lexicon/g1391/esv/mgnt/0-1/.

So yes, we *can* be one by the powerful and majestic glory of Almighty God!

So, how can we achieve this lofty vision that Jesus prayed for his believers?

The next chapter offers God himself as the answer. He is the Father, who is *for us*, the Son, who is God *with us*, and the Holy Spirit, who dwells *in us*. If you are curious what that means (and I hope you are), then keep these pages turning.

DEVOTIONAL REFLECTIONS (INDIVIDUALLY OR IN SMALL GROUPS)

1. Write down a few analogies that describe (a) your perception of God and (b) your relationship with God (in small groups, share your lists).

2. In what ways has God shown his desire to be known by you? Be as specific as possible, including dates, locations, circumstances, etc. (in small groups, share your lists).

3. Read Acts 17:16–31. Use your favorite translation plus a paraphrase like The Passion Translation. Which verses (or words) in Paul's address draw your attention? Spend five to ten minutes highlighting them in your Bible or writing them down.

4. Your current pursuit of a relationship with God is (a) active, (b) on hold, or (c) abandoned? Write down your honest introspection (in small groups, share your reflections).

5. What about your current pursuit of relationships with others in Christ (same a, b, and c as above)? Write down your honest introspection (in small groups, share your reflections).

6. Prayer focus: "God, reshape my pursuit of relationships in Christ to mirror your pursuit of me."

7. Song of reflection: "Goodness of God" as performed by Cece Winans.

A REFLECTION

My few experiences with church collaboration have been richest when they were built on (or resulted in) relationships of trust. Even some collaborations that never materialized into the desired programs or events still became trusted relationships with diverse church leaders who became friends. In reflection, I see that a common thread was not trying to force a collaboration of our own design. Instead, God taught me (sometimes the hard way) to look for the places where he was at work and to join him in that. Often that resulted in results beyond what we could have asked or imagined! From mission trips to a neighborhood center to helping with city zoning approvals to community service projects, when one church lets another truly lead and then is willing to join in, great things can happen! Several of these trusting collaborative relationships were diverse ones, but the nature and focus of our relationship was always the same—our mission as the church to help as many as possible to know and follow Jesus. And as I think about a point in this book about pastors as shepherds with defined job descriptions, I can see now that I had the "advantage" of not being a pastor but was instead an elder and lay leader. This gave me the freedom to pursue collaboration. I am just grateful for my church pastors (including the author of this book) being clear advocates and champions of church collaboration!

Tom Greene
Shoreline Church
Monterey, CA

Chapter 3

Imitating the Trinity
(The Illustrations)

A pulse you feel when listening to music. It measures the passing of time (tempo) and helps musicians perform together and read rhythms.

—Beat (music theory)

HOW CAN OUR COLLABORATION MIRROR GOD?

The Trinity's uniqueness and perfect community is both a theological reality and the ideal model for local church collaboration. But how can regional church collaboration possibly mirror the vastness of the Godhead's loving community? Let me hone that question:

Which renowned attributes of the Father, Son, and Spirit can our relational unity in Christ emulate?

Here is my answer with three illustrations of God:

Collaboration imitates how the Father is for us, the Son is with us, and the Holy Spirit lives in us.

This answer comes from a communion devotional I shared at the church where I currently serve. Most believers understand why we talk about Jesus during holy communion.

> And as they were eating, he took bread, and after blessing it broke it and gave it to them, and said, "Take; this is my body." And he took a cup, and when he had given thanks, he gave it to them, and they all drank of it. And he said to them, "This is my blood of the covenant, which is poured out for many." (Mark 14:22–24)

The bread and wine analogize the redemptive work of the Son of God. Most Christians practice the sacramental remembrance of the body and blood of Jesus when they eat and drink the Lord's Supper.

Sometimes the Father makes cameos during the Good Friday and Easter services. But for whatever reason, communion devotionals in evangelical churches are typically bereft of the work of the Father and the Spirit at the cross and the empty tomb. Instead, we honor the Son of God's redemptive work while omitting the fullness of God's participation. As for the Holy Spirit, we act as if he was waiting on Pentecost for his big entrance in the upper room.

As I prepared my devotional comments on that particular occasion, I asked myself, Who is the Father at the Lord's Supper, the Son at the Passover meal, and the Holy Spirit at the communion table? My answer was a breathtaking revelation:

God is the Father, who is for us, the Son, who is with us, and the Spirit, who lives in us.

I soon discovered that these three caricatures provide tangible guides to help kingdom partnerships mirror the Trinity.

Before We Move On . . .

Some of you might be thinking, "Wait! The Spirit isn't the only divine presence living in his people. Don't the Father, Son, and Holy Spirit all live in his people?"

The answer is yes. The apostle Paul taught that the fullness of God was pleased to dwell in Jesus (Col 1:19) and that the same Christ lives in us (Gal 2:20). Since all of God lives in Christ and Christ lives in us, that means all of God lives in us.

However, this theological truth does not derail my portraiture of God. He is the Father, who is always *for* his kids; he is the Son, who physically walked on earth *with* his people; and he is the Holy Spirit sent as a comforter to dwell *in* us. When believers work together, we emulate the relational community of the Father, who is for us, the Son, who is God with us, and the Spirit, who is God in us. Each thumbnail sketch provides vital visual lessons on how our collaboration can mirror God.

Let us look at each beautiful snapshot of the Trinity as our path forward for practicing unity.

THE FATHER IS GOD WHO IS "FOR US"

God the Father is the one who is *for us.*

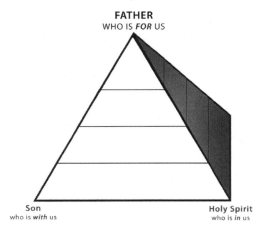

The psalmist David described Yahweh in the following way: "Father of the fatherless and protector of widows is God in his holy habitation" (Ps 68:5). The prophet Isaiah wrote, "For you are our Father, though Abraham does not know us, and Israel does not acknowledge us; you, O Lord, are our Father, our Redeemer from of old is your name" (Isa 63:16). Listen to Jesus describe the Father, who is *for us.*

What do you think? If a man has a hundred sheep, and one of them has gone astray, does he not leave the ninety-nine on the mountains and go in search of the one that went astray? And if he finds it, truly, I say to you, he rejoices over it more than over the ninety-nine that never went astray. So it is not the will of my Father who is in heaven that one of these little ones should perish. (Matt 18:12–14)

Or which one of you, if his son asks him for bread, will give him a stone? Or if he asks for a fish, will give him a serpent? If you then, who are evil, know how to give good gifts to your children, how much more will your Father who is in heaven give good things to those who ask him! (Matt 7:9–11)

The Father is who God is. He wants believers to love and adore him as a Father: "See what kind of love the Father has given to us, that we should be called children of God; and so, we are" (1 John 3:1). In addition, the heart of the gospel lies in the truth that God, who is the Father, gave the world his very best—his son (John 3:16). It is the Father who stands on the porch waiting for his lost son to return home and receive a lavish welcome from him (Luke 15:11–32). These few passages are indicative of how the Scriptures reveal God as the Father, who is *for us*.

APPLICATION: THE CHURCH SHOULD ROOT FOR ONE ANOTHER

Local churches ought to cheer one another on. In doing so, we reflect how the Father roots for us, his sons and daughters. He loves his kids, and his kids ought to love one another. He cares for his people, and his people ought to care for one another. He sacrificed his Son for the world's salvation, so neighborhood churches ought to esteem each other's agendas and preferences over their own.

Peter Greer, Chris Horst, and Jill Heisey agree. They described the purpose of their book *Rooting for Rivals* as "an invitation for faith-based organizations to be known for outrageous generosity and openhandedness, as we collectively pursue a calling higher than any one organization's agenda. It's an invitation to live not as warring clans, but as people of a united kingdom."[1] The writers further challenge churches "to reject comparison and rivalry and pursue collaboration and friendship."[2] This challenge applies to individual believers as well as local communities of faith.

What Do They Mean by Rivals?

Greer, Horst, and Heisey examined the state of the worldwide church using imagery of clans (siloed churches) vs. kingdom (collaborative churches). They define "clan" as "everything and everyone inside our organization's boundaries."[3] "Kingdom" means "where we submit our efforts to God's reigning authority and become co-laborers in a shared mission to bring heaven to earth."[4] Their clans vs. kingdom analogy is a warning for congregations. An honest self-examination will reveal an accurate depiction of your church culture.

A famous example of rivals rooting for one another is the shocking partnership created in 1997 between desktop-computer rivals Apple and Microsoft. Steve Jobs returned to Apple after being fired by their board of directors in 1985. His primary task was to save the company on the verge of bankruptcy. Jobs implemented several company-wide changes, but the standout was the deal he brokered with rival Bill Gates and the Microsoft Corporation. At Macworld Boston 1997, Jobs informed attendees that Apple had entered into a strategic partnership with Microsoft.[5] Then the stunned audience heard the sentence that changed the course of their company forever: "We have to let go of this notion that for

1. Greer et al., *Rooting for Rivals*, 23.

2. Greer et al., *Rooting for Rivals*, 23.

3. Greer et al., *Rooting for Rivals*, 63.

4. Greer et al., *Rooting for Rivals*, 64.

5. Jobs, "Macworld Boston 1997."

Apple to win, Microsoft has to lose."[6] Apple bought into this progressive way of thinking, and Apple not only recovered but grew exponentially with the help of strategic partners like Microsoft and Oracle.

That famous sentence encapsulates a central message for this project: the body of Christ must let go of the notion that for your church to win, other congregations have to lose.

When collaboration mirrors the Trinity, siloed congregations cheer for one another in their gospel endeavors. In so doing, our unity in Christ resembles God the Father, who is *for us*.

THE SON IS GOD WHO IS "WITH US"

The Son of God is the one who is Immanuel, God *with us*. He is tangible proof that God wants to be known by humanity.

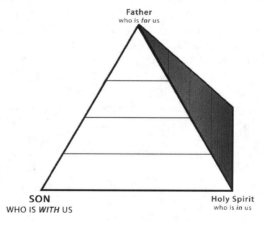

In the narrative of Jesus' birth, Matthew quotes Isaiah's messianic prophecy (Isa 7:14): "All this took place to fulfill what the Lord had spoken by the prophet: 'Behold, the virgin shall conceive and bear a son, and they shall call his name Immanuel' (which means, God with us)" (Matt 1:22–23). John speaks of the Word, Jesus, existing in the beginning. This same Word, who is God,

6. Dernbach, "MacWorld Boston 1997," para. 1.

"became flesh and dwelt among us, and we have seen his glory, glory as of the only Son from the Father, full of grace and truth" (John 1:14). He continues, "No one has ever seen God; the only God, who is at the Father's side, he has made him known" (John 1:18). He also quotes Jesus' testimony about his divinity: "I and the Father are one" (John 10:30).

The Jews have always known Yahweh as the God who brought them out of the land of Egypt. No wonder they wanted to kill Jesus when they heard his claim of divinity.

> The Jews answered him, "Are we not right in saying that you are a Samaritan and have a demon?" Jesus answered, "I do not have a demon, but I honor my Father, and you dishonor me. Yet I do not seek my own glory; there is One who seeks it, and he is the judge. Truly, truly, I say to you, if anyone keeps my word, he will never see death." The Jews said to him, "Now we know that you have a demon! Abraham died, as did the prophets, yet you say, 'If anyone keeps my word, he will never taste death.' Are you greater than our father Abraham, who died? And the prophets died! Who do you make yourself out to be?" Jesus answered, "If I glorify myself, my glory is nothing. It is my Father who glorifies me, of whom you say, 'He is our God.' But you have not known him. I know him. If I were to say that I do not know him, I would be a liar like you, but I do know him, and I keep his word. Your father Abraham rejoiced that he would see my day. He saw it and was glad." So, the Jews said to him, "You are not yet fifty years old, and have you seen Abraham?" Jesus said to them, "Truly, truly, I say to you, before Abraham was, I am." So, they picked up stones to throw at him, but Jesus hid himself and went out of the temple. (John 8:48–59)

Notice the breakdown of Jesus' claims in this text.

* In verse 49, he claims that God is his Father.

* In verse 51, Jesus says that he gives eternal life.

* In verse 54, he claims that God the Father glorifies him.

* In verses 55 and 56, he claims that he knows the Father intimately and that their Jewish father Abraham revered him.

* In verse 58, Jesus claims that he is the same "I AM" of the Hebrew scriptures (the one and only, living God).

In other words, Jesus affirmed what the biblical writers said. Therefore, he, the Son, is God.

After the resurrected Jesus said his goodbyes to his disciples, they watched him ascend into the heavens: "And they worshiped him and returned to Jerusalem with great joy, and were continually in the temple blessing God" (Luke 24:52–53). As Jews, they reserved worship for God alone. Yet, they worshiped Jesus. Why? The disciples finally believed that he was Immanuel, God *with us*.

APPLICATION: THE CHURCH SHOULD BE WITH ONE ANOTHER ON MISSION

The Son of God showed his love for humanity by coming to earth to live *with us* and by sacrificing his life to save the world's people. God's people reflect his amazing love whenever they intentionally leave their comfort zones to be *with one another*. He never intended for us to live life in isolation.

* Just like Jesus walked with his disciples, believers ought to walk in fellowship *with one another*.

* Just like Jesus showed patience with his followers, his church ought to be patient *with one another*.

* Just like Jesus had compassion on the crowds, his body ought to show mercy to and walk arm in arm with *her neighbors and communities*.

The Son perfectly modeled a sacrificial mindset in living *with us* (Phil 2:4–8). Therefore, when local churches determine to be *with one another* on the gospel mission, they will become a more united, healthier church and a more accurate representation of her God.

We Can Work Together

Phill Butler's *Well Connected* is a helpful tool for this subject. His opening challenge to the twenty-first-century church is that "God's people can work together. Even more, working together, they are accomplishing miraculous things—things that would never happen if they were working independently."[7] Butler observes "many good people doing good kingdom things but generally not actively coordinating their efforts."[8] Butler's comments are necessary because of the enormity of the gospel mission. He asks, "If we want to see real spiritual breakthroughs in our region, is there anything of importance we can only do together rather than continuing to work individually?"[9] His firm answer: "Simply put, no single ministry or individual can ever hope to 'reach a city.' Only by working together could the dream ever come true."[10]

There is an undeniable logic to Butler's argument, yet stories about victorious local church collaborations are rare. Why is this? He rather bluntly suggests that the problem is a systemic spiritual defect: "The brokenness in the church, the divisions that abound, and our consistent resistance to the God design of restored relationships and practical unity is [the church's] truly great sin."[11] Like myself, Butler believes that the church of Jesus Christ ought never to be a worldwide network of siloed organizations having no connections or strategic fellowship with one another.

On the contrary, he helps his readers identify the influence of cultural individualism in the body of Christ. Individualism, especially in the West, is a yeast permeating all aspects of society, including God's church. Butler observes that "the Western cultural perspective of individualism and quick results powerfully affects our view of scripture itself, how individuals come to Christ, how discipleship occurs, and how effective strategies of evangelism and

7. Butler, *Well Connected*, 1.
8. Butler, *Well Connected*, 3.
9. Butler, *Well Connected*, 5–6.
10. Butler, *Well Connected*, 273.
11. Butler, *Well Connected*, 6.

service are carried out."[12] Butler is highlighting how individualism is a core value in our culture. Biblically, however, the church was never intended to mirror or resemble culture. Instead, the church is a nation of people called out from the culture by the gospel in order to—with the help of Jesus Christ—build our lives to mirror him. Butler's indictment of individualism in the church is spot on and biblical. He argues that life in Christ always flourishes in the context of a community of believers. I completely agree. When collaboration mirrors the Trinity, believers and faith communities alike commit to ongoing relationships with each other. The resulting relational rhythms honor Christ's intended design for his church. Such a culture reflects the heart of God—the Son, who is *with us.*

THE HOLY SPIRIT IS GOD "IN US"

The Holy Spirit is God who dwells *in us.*

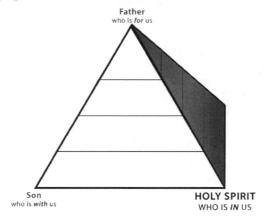

He was there at the beginning of creation: "The earth was without form and void, and darkness was over the face of the deep. And the Spirit of God was hovering over the face of the waters" (Gen 1:2).

12. Butler, *Well Connected*, 60.

God's very nature is spirit: "God is spirit, and those who worship him must worship in spirit and truth" (John 4:24).

Jesus sent his disciples into the mission field with these words of preparation: "When they deliver you over, do not be anxious how you are to speak or what you are to say, for what you are to say will be given to you in that hour. For it is not you who speak, but the Spirit of your Father speaking through you" (Matt 10:19–20).

Notice how Jesus prepared them to embody the Holy Spirit literally: "And I will ask the Father, and he will give you another Helper, to be with you forever" (John 14:16). "When the Spirit of truth comes, he will guide you into all the truth, for he will not speak on his own authority, but whatever he hears, he will speak, and he will declare to you the things that are to come. He will glorify me, for he will take what is mine and declare it to you. All that the Father has is mine; therefore, I said that he will take what is mine and declare it to you" (John 16:12–15).

Paul taught the Corinthians the following: "Do you not know that you are God's temple and that God's Spirit dwells in you?" (1 Cor 3:16). "Or do you not know that your body is a temple of the Holy Spirit within you, whom you have from God? You are not your own, for you were bought with a price. So glorify God in your body" (1 Cor 6:19–20).

He taught the Ephesians, "And do not get drunk with wine, for that is debauchery, but be filled with the Spirit" (Eph 5:18).

No one is capable of understanding the wisdom of God without the Spirit: "These things God has revealed to us through the Spirit. For the Spirit searches everything, even the depths of God. For who knows a person's thoughts except the spirit of that person, which is in him? So also no one comprehends the thoughts of God except the Spirit of God" (1 Cor 2:10–11).

These biblical texts and many others testify about the work of the Spirit *in us*. He creates, moves, indwells, loves, inspired Scripture (2 Tim 3:16), guarantees our salvation (Eph 1:13–14), and confirms the Father's love for the Son throughout eternity. The Holy Spirit is God, the one who is *in us*

APPLICATION: MEMBERS OF THE CHURCH SHOULD REMAIN IN ONE ANOTHER'S HEARTS

The Holy Spirit came to live and dwell *in us*. He insists that we see and treat every believing congregation worldwide as part of our family. His guidance creates the impetus for collaboration between various congregations of the one church. When kingdom alliances produce relational trust, the participants encounter increasing love and care for one another over time.

When the Spirit in us and the same Spirit in them illuminates our unity, we begin to change our perspective on how we live with the other congregations around town. We will want to pray more often for one another. We will inquire more often about one another out of heartfelt concern that deepens through collaboration. Just like the Holy Spirit dwells in his people, we will begin to remember one another and grow in love for one another as we become more unified. In a real sense, Christian brothers and sisters remain in the hearts of other believers. The Holy Spirit perfectly modeled intentionality in remaining *in us*. When believers discover how collaboration keeps the lives of their brothers and sisters lingering in their hearts, they will be encouraged to practice the unity of the Spirit as a normative demonstration of the gospel.

THE EARLY CHURCH MODELED COLLABORATION

Whereas unity is the relationship among believers that mirrors the Trinity, collaboration is a practice of the church that manifests the unity of the body of Christ (1 Cor 12). Here are a few New Testament examples of collaboration.

From the beginning of the church, Jesus followers were a self-giving community of faith:

> And they devoted themselves to the apostles' teaching and the fellowship, to the breaking of bread and the prayers. And awe came upon every soul, and many wonders and signs were being done through the apostles. And all who believed were together and had all things

in common. And they were selling their possessions and belongings and distributing the proceeds to all, as any had need. And day by day, attending the temple together and breaking bread in their homes, they received their food with glad and generous hearts, praising God and having favor with all the people. And the Lord added to their number day by day those who were being saved. (Acts 2:42–47)

The newly committed Jesus followers understood that they needed one another. They wanted to help each other with their day-to-day needs. So they generously committed themselves to be together in Christ.

First Corinthians 16 begins with a beautiful example of economic collaboration:

Now concerning the collection for the saints: as I directed the churches of Galatia, so you also are to do. On the first day of every week, each of you is to put something aside and store it up, as he may prosper so that there will be no collecting when I come. And when I arrive, I will send those whom you accredit by letter to carry your gift to Jerusalem. If it seems advisable that I should go also, they will accompany me. (1 Cor 16:1–4)

In this text, several congregations throughout Galatia joined together with Paul to bless the struggling believers in Jerusalem. This collective invitation to the Corinthians came from his confidence that they would gladly participate in the kingdom work (2 Cor 9:1–5). Paul was the visionary leader facilitating the collaboration. Their combined efforts model how congregations can work together in Christ.

In Acts 6, the apostles commissioned seven men "to deliver a marginalized community from an injustice," meaning the overlooked widows (Acts 6:1–7).[13] The reality is that "the Twelve gathered all the disciples together" to work collaboratively in service (Acts 6:2a). In his blog reflection of this text, Greg Dueker believes that the apostles illustrated healthy collaboration to resolve this

13. Dueker, "Spirit-Filled Seven," para. 1.

dilemma. First, they "didn't micromanage the situation but released the selection of those who would address the problem to
those who would be served by them."[14] Second, in verse 3, men
were chosen from their midst, "the first indications of the rapid incorporation of indigenous leadership in order to correct this over-
sight in the care for the poor."[15] Third, "the apostles called for a full
team (of seven men) to face the challenge," which meant they were
serious about correcting "a social injustice."[16] Fourth, the apostles
appointed those who were chosen, giving them both responsibility
and authority. As Dueker notes, "responsibility without authority
only brings frustration."[17] Lastly, the apostles stayed on track by
devoting themselves "to prayer and to the ministry of the word"
(Acts 6:4). Congregations in the same cities could use this as a
healthy model for collaboration.

An example of two culturally different congregations working toward unity is the Jerusalem council. Paul, Barnabas, and the
apostles and elders met to debate active Judaizing teachings: "But
some men came down from Judea and were teaching the brothers,
'Unless you are circumcised according to the custom of Moses,
you cannot be saved'" (Acts 15:1). James told the Jewish assembly
they should "not trouble those of the Gentiles who turn to God but
should write to them to abstain from the things polluted by idols,
and from sexual immorality, and from what has been strangled,
and from blood" (Acts 15:19b–20). A subsequent letter was composed by these Jewish believers to instruct, encourage, and build
unity in Christ with the Gentile believers in Antioch (Acts 15:23–
29): "And when [the Gentile believers] had read it, they rejoiced
because of its encouragement" (Acts 15:31). Thus, what began as
a dispute among Jewish believers and a burden among Gentile believers resulted in one community lovingly rooting for the other.

Paul's missionary journeys were collaborative. Several texts
talk about "Paul and his companions" visiting and planting

14. Dueker, "Spirit-Filled Seven," para. 4.

15. Dueker, "Spirit-Filled Seven," para. 4.

16. Dueker, "Spirit-Filled Seven," para. 4.

17. Dueker, "Spirit-Filled Seven," para. 4.

churches from Judea to Macedonia (Acts 13:13, 16:6, and 17:1). They partnered together in a shared vision of the gospel mission.

These are examples of how the first-century church saw collaboration as more than a soft suggestion. They were obeying Jesus' prayer: "Holy Father, keep them in your name, which you have given me, that they may be one, even as we are one" (John 17:11). This prayer was their pursued rhythm in Christ.

SUMMARY OF HOW OUR COLLABORATION MIRRORS THE TRINITY

The Trinity, who is first and foremost relational, is the perfect diverse community. Our collaboration, then, should imitate three illustrations of God: the way the Father is *for us*, the Son is *with us*, and the Holy Spirit lives *in us*. Below are ways that our active unity can mirror him.

God	Three Illustrations	Ways to Mirror the Trinity
The Father	is *for us*	Like the Father, local churches should root *for one another* and never be rivals.
The Son	is *with us*	Like the Son, local churches should partner *with one another* on the gospel mission to bless their cities.
The Holy Spirit	is *in us*	Like the Holy Spirit, we should bind together by our mutual love for God and, in doing so, remain *in one another's hearts*.

DEVOTIONAL REFLECTIONS
(INDIVIDUALLY OR IN SMALL GROUPS)

1. Write down the names of people who are (a) spiritually rooting *for* you, (b) walking *with* you, and (c) keeping you *in* their thoughts and prayers. What are the indicators of their support (in small groups, share your responses)?

2. Who are *you* spiritually (a) rooting *for*, (b) walking *with*, and (c) keeping *in* your thoughts and prayers? What are the indicators of your support (in small groups, share your responses)?

3. Read Deut 31:6, Isa 41:10, and 2 Cor 1:3–4. Use your favorite translation. Which verses (or phrases) draw your attention? Spend five to ten minutes highlighting them in your Bible or writing them down.

4. In what practical ways has God been (a) rooting *for* you, (b) walking *with* you, and (c) living *in* you? Be as specific as possible, including dates, locations, circumstances, etc. (in small groups, share your lists).

5. Consider how your church might mirror God in your relationships with other churches in your city. Then, write down a few practical ideas (in small groups, share your thoughts).

6. Prayer focus: "Father, Son, and Spirit, align my heart to love others the way you love one another."

7. Song of reflection: "Tell Me Something I Don't Know" as performed by Acappella.

An Encouragement

Congratulations on your new book. I thank God that he is working with each one of us and guiding us every day. I pray that the book will be used as a tool to glorify his name and spread the gospel around the nation. He is our hope everlasting.

"Finally, brothers and sisters, rejoice! Strive for full restoration, encourage one another, be of one mind, live in peace. And the God of love and peace will be with you" (2 Cor 13:11).

新しい本の出版をおめでとうございます。神様はいつも私達に働き、導いてくださることを感謝します。この本が神様の栄光を表し福音が世よに伝わる手段として用いられるようお祈りいたします。神様は私達の希望であり、永遠な方です。

「終わりに兄弟たち、喜びなさい。完全な者になりなさい。慰めを受けなさい。一つ心になりなさい。平和を保ちなさい。そうすれば、愛と平和の神はあなた方と共にいてくださいます。」コリント人への手紙第二章13節

Peace and love,
Seiko Tozaki
Machida Christian Center
Tokyo, Japan

Chapter 4

Back to the One

Literally translates to 'from the head' and it instructs the musicians to return to the beginning or to repeat a section of music.

—DA CAPO (ITALIAN MUSICAL TERM)

IF YOU READ THE introduction and allowed it to sink in, chances are that you want the twenty-first-century church to be farther along on the unity thing. Thanks for hanging with me, because I have more information to share that may bless your ministry.

THE "ONE"

I grew up listening to all kinds of music on long-play albums, or LPs, single-track 45 records, 8-track tapes, and cassette tapes. Dad helped me develop my musical palette by letting me listen to all kinds of music. We played music from artists that had no apparent stylistic connection whatsoever. Dad would crank up Bobby "Blue" Bland's "I Pity the Fool," followed by "Burt Bacharach's Greatest Hits." As a kid, I cut my teeth on everything Motown, Sam Cooke and the Soul Stirrers, the Beach Boys, the Mighty Clouds of Joy, and a list too long to share in this setting. My teenaged musical palette expanded to vocal-harmony groups like the Manhattan Transfer, Earth, Wind & Fire, the Nylons, Acappella, Take 6, and others. Every week I watched television shows like *Soul Train*, *Don Kirshner's Rock Concert*, *American Bandstand*, and even *Hee Haw*. And the more I learned the language of music, the more I saw how diverse styles shared commonalities. One particular characteristic was universal, whether R&B or Jazz, Rock or Hip Hop, Country or Gospel. And the legendary artist who exploited it best was the "Godfather of Soul."

James Brown changed the landscape of rhythm and blues by stripping down the complexity of music and emphasizing the first beat of every measure—the "one."

Let me try to illustrate this.

Count out loud "one–two–three–four" in a repeated cycle. Say the word "one" louder than the rest. Notice the emphasis placed on the one (first beat) in the series (measure). For my rocker friends, the one lands on the first "we" and the "rock you" in Queen's "*We–will–we–will–rock* you."

For James Brown, soul music was all about "the one."

He was never classically trained and never developed a reputation as a musical prodigy. Yet Brown's songs have been sampled by more artists than any musician in recorded music history.[1] They appreciated the infectious way he highlighted the "one" (the lead-off beat in a song). He would yell "hit me," and his band knew to go back to the *one* regardless of their current location in the composition. But how was that possible?

The "one" is like the north star of music. It is a focused point to guide musicians while they perform. Band players can recalibrate to it whenever they get a wee bit out of sync. Their realignment is possible because the "one" always comes back around sooner or later. Artists like Chick Corea (old school) and Snarky Puppy (new school) play complex songs with multiple musicians. Their fusion styles are only possible with the universal constant of "the one." It helps musicians with diverse instruments to play with precision.

1. See Gordon, "James Brown."

No wonder the Godfather of Soul could tell the world, "I feel good!"

Hoping that all my nonmusical readers are still with me, here is my point: the worldwide church of Jesus Christ must, for all times, get back to the "one."

BACK TO THE ONE

The "one," for the sake of this thesis, refers to the loving, relational community of the triune God. It is time to place greater emphasis on how to mirror him, just like James Brown popularized with the lead-off beat in soul music.

Let us not sugarcoat our situation. Church segregation and disunity are actualities, regardless of our theological aspirations. Evangelicals may use terms like "sister congregations" or "unity of believers" to verbalize our doctrine but are slow to admit our "out of sync" reality. As a result, we look like quarrelsome musicians who know the music but sound horrible playing together. And we wonder why the listening audience does not want to subscribe to our Spotify station.

Ask yourself how your dogmas performed in 2020.

* Did your values of individualism and autonomy display the love of Christ?

* Did your expressed politics convince friends and neighbors to become believers?

* Did you encourage or support local congregations hurting during the pandemic?

* Did your "correct" theology bless families in under-resourced neighborhoods?

* Did your social media blasts move the needle toward justice, love, kindness, and mercy?

My brothers and sisters, *we have arrived where we are by doing what we have done.* Yes, we are all on the gospel mission. But boy, we sure could use a recalibration to help us play better together! We need to get back to the "one" and lock into some new rhythms.

REJECTING THE CURRENT NORMAL

Not only does Mark DeYmaz reject our current normal, but he believes the culture of today's church discredits believers from sharing the good news in their cities.

> The systemic segregation of the local church unintentionally undermines the credibility of our witness in the broader community and greatly impedes our ability to influence those outside a specific demographic group upon whom the church was likely established and to which it continues to cater. Mere proclamation or explanation of the gospel, then, without an observable local church witness of God's love for diverse people is no longer an option, no longer enough to win hearts and minds in these changing times. To do that the church must fully embrace the ministry of reconciliation, and in doing so demonstrate the power of the gospel to bring diverse men and women together by the blood of Christ through the cross (2 Cor 5:11–21; Eph 2:11–16). Simultaneously, it must also advance justice, love mercy, and walk humbly with God among the people of the city.[2]

The unity of believers is not a trending program or a flavor-of-the-month church-growth strategy. Instead, God designed congregations to be, as DeYmaz says, the "local church witness of God's love for diverse people."[3] Anything less is a familiar segregated church doing what it has always done—achieving only a shadow of what it could be and do.

2. DeYmaz, *Disruption*, 32–33.
3. DeYmaz, *Disruption*, 33.

UNION VS. UNITY

Several of my non-Black Christian brothers and sisters inquire why the subject of unity seems to lead routinely to a conversation about race. To paraphrase their concern, "Is not our *union* with Christ good enough?" They seem to be saying that all Christians live under the same spiritual umbrella because we individually follow him. "I'm a Christian, and you're a Christian; therefore, we have *unity* with Christ." That makes sense, right? However, let me press into that idea with a thought exercise.

My dad would often illustrate the difference between *union* and *unity*. Take two cats, tie their tails together, and throw them over your backyard clothesline. The resulting action is *union*, but it sure isn't *unity*! His point was that our connections to Christ individually do not ensure that we desire relationships with one another. If our independent links to Christ were "good enough" to achieve unity, why did Jesus make an effort to pray that we would be one?

Perhaps he anticipated friction among believers, even racial segregation perpetrated in his name. A case in point involves the history of an African American church in Portland, Oregon:

> The church was originally located on the Northwest of Portland, at Broadway and Everett. In 1921, to get the church on the "proper side of town," the Ku Klux Klan donated some lumber to help the church relocate to the Northeast side on the corner of NE Schuyler and 1st Avenue.[4]

Does that phrase "the proper side of town" communicate unity to you? Sure, some progress in race relations has improved in our world, but the task is far from complete. The truth of Dr. King's indictment on the American church is still painful and laser accurate:

> I think it is one of the tragedies of our nation, one of the shameful tragedies, that eleven o'clock on Sunday

---

4. "History of Mt. Olivet," para. 1.

morning is one of the most segregated hours, if not the most segregated hours, in Christian America."[5]

We preach that we are one, but honestly, do we look like it? This twenty-first-century world, especially younger generations, turns away from our verbal message because it does not visibly match our lived-out experiences. This unfortunate reality is more than regrettable; it is heartbreaking. Why? Our Christian dissonance persuades outsiders that we have little or nothing to offer their lives. So, they seek answers elsewhere. Remember when Jesus asked Peter if he would leave his master? He responded, "Lord, to whom shall we go? You have the words of eternal life, and we have believed, and have come to know, that you are the Holy One of God" (John 6:68–69). We possess the only real answers that lead to abundant life—Jesus Christ. But what does that matter if our relational discord hinders people from seeking Christ and perhaps finding him?

Like I said, heartbreaking.

I want to challenge believers to acknowledge our *union with Christ* but to know that the goal is *unity in Christ.*

If you believe that you are in sync with Christ while firmly remaining distant from others in Christ, you are wrong: "If anyone boasts, 'I love God,' and goes right on hating his brother or sister, thinking nothing of it, he is a liar. If he won't love the person he can see, how can he love the God he can't see? The command we have from Christ is blunt: Loving God includes loving people. You've got to love both" (1 John 4:20–21 MSG).

Believers connected to Christ need positive relationships with one another. Those ties should lead to honest conversations about who we are as people: hurts, joys, experiences, differences, similarities, ministry dreams, wounds, betrayal, and so on. They also prompt valuable dialogue about race, equality, and justice. These are the behaviors that bridge the gap between union and unity. Jesus calls us to be one, not one-ish!

5. King, Jr., "Interview," para. 55.

ONE-ISH

Black-ish is a brilliant television show. It delineates the vast continuum of Black culture depicted in our history, experiences, melanin shades, and so on. The "ish" in the show title gives the nod to this reality. Its central message is that everyone on our ethnic and cultural continuum is Black. If you have interracial parents and one of them is African American, you are Black. If an African American child is adopted into a family of different racial origin, that child is Black. None of them are any less Black than other African Americans. No one is actually Black-ish.

I understand this continuum, which explains why I never speak definitively on behalf of all Black people about all subjects.

Therein lies a curious tension related to this discussion—

Nobody has a goal to be "ish."

I am not a Christian-ish pastor.

You are not my spiritual family-ish.

And the body of Christ should never be satisfied at being one-ish.

Some of you may struggle with my assessment of today's church. Maybe you attribute unity to the many denominations and church brands in your city. Perhaps in your mind, our public battles do not amount to full-on disunity. Maybe you feel that Dr. King's analysis of the segregated church is overblown. If so, stay with me a bit longer and let us play a quick game.

ONE OR ONE-ISH?

Here is a short exercise called "One or One-ish?" Below are nine true-to-life church scenarios in your city. I consider all of them one-ish (at best). However, you make the call for each scene. Do they exemplify the body of Christ as being one or "sort of" one? As you go through the list, feel free to add actual cases or instances in your city that help you engage in this exercise.

Scenario One: There are hundreds of autonomous churches in your city.

59

Scenario Two: Dozen of churches assemble within a one-mile radius of your church campus; you have never met any of their members.

Scenario Three: The Department of Parks and Recreation has a database of faith-based organizations in your city. Unfortunately, your longstanding church is not in their database.

Scenario Four: The last time your church prayed for another church in your community was . . .

Scenario Five: A struggling church closed and used its liquidated assets to build a new church across town—one block away from *your* struggling church.

Scenario Six: Four churches in your large metro city have pastor vacancies; you discovered them on a Christian employment website.

Scenario Seven: A well-funded church plant launched a year ago in the shopping mall near your church campus. You found out about it two weeks ago.

Scenario Eight: A new family came to your church because they like your preaching better than the pastor of their previous church.

Scenario Nine: The last time you studied the Bible with someone from another church was . . .

Scenario Ten: Add your example here.

If you are tracking with the one-ish idea, then revisit this chapter's initial analogy. Great music relies on vocalists and instrumentalists having the same "one," or point of reference, throughout the entire performance or recording. But more than that, they must also play *together*. Precision play can still sound horrible if individual musicians perform as if no one else is in the band!

Here is the mathematical formula: believers locked to the Father, Son, and Holy Spirit + loving connections to one another = one.

Our unity in Christ requires both connections. This formula embedded into the lifeblood of local churches helps the body of Christ be one and not just one-ish.

MOVING TOWARD THE BRIDGE

The loving community of the Father, Son, and Holy Spirit is the place where our kingdom partnerships must sync. The next chapter shares four beautiful rhythms of collaboration that reflect the nature of the Trinity. These principles can position local churches to participate collaboratively in the *missio Dei*.[6]

Turn the page and head toward the bridge.

DEVOTIONAL REFLECTIONS
(INDIVIDUALLY OR IN SMALL GROUPS)

1. Recount a time when you felt out of sync with Christ. What helped you get back to the "one"? Be as specific as possible (in small groups, share your testimonies).

2. Read Rom 8:28–39. Use your favorite translation plus a paraphrase like Peterson's The Message. Which verses (or phrases) draw your attention? Spend five to ten minutes highlighting them in your Bible or writing them down.

3. If you were visiting a new church, what indicators would convince you that they are part of the body of Christ? Spend several minutes writing them down (in small groups, share and compare your responses).

4. When visitors attend *your* church, what obvious ways can show your connection to the body of Christ? Spend several minutes writing them down (in small groups, share your indicators).

5. In what practical ways could the local churches collaboratively bless your city? Write down your dream list (in small groups, share your ideas).

6. Prayer focus: "Triune God, make your people one as you are one."

6. *Missio Dei* is a Latin phrase often used in missiology that is rendered into English as "mission of God" (Brisco, "Missio Dei," para. 1).

7. Song of reflection: "By Our Love" as performed by for King & Country.

TWO PRAYERS

Father God,

We thank you for your love that was poured out for us in the suffering and death of your Son, Jesus, who is the Christ. We thank you for your adoption as sons and daughters and that you have sealed that adoption with the Holy Spirit. We ask, Lord, that you might unite the hearts of all your children around this truth, whether Black or White, Eastern or Western, expressive or reserved, male or female, denominational or non-denominational, rich or poor, Jew or Gentile. Give us a heart of humility that we might encourage one another as the family we are in Christ. May the world know that we are lovers and followers of Jesus by the love we have for one another. May we be one as you and the Son are one.

In the name of our Master and Savior, Jesus, we pray. Amen.

Joel King
Lead Pastor
Trinity Church of Sunnyvale
Sunnyvale, CA

Dear Lord,
May I be compassionate;
I am a child of your mercy.
May I be generous;
You have given me so much.
May I overlook and forget;
I am forgiven—you spared me.
Together, every face, every name,
Alike, we praise you.
Together, not alone, not apart,
Brothers, sisters.
Together, Father, we are one;
We share your presence.
Heal us, bind us as one.

Paul Hastings
Trinity Church of Sunnyvale
Sunnyvale, CA

Chapter 5

Four Rhythms of Collaboration

Simultaneous sounding of musical notes/pitches that produce chords that are pleasing to listen to.

—Harmony (music theory)

Throughout this material, I have discussed my thesis in a variety of ways. Let me now present it emphatically.

THE THESIS

The thesis of this project is that local church collaboration should be a normative practice of unity that mirrors the Trinity. This type of collaboration seeks to reflect four traits of the Trinity's loving unity: *relationship, trust, diversity, and inclusion.*

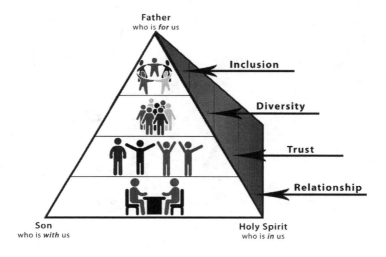

Four Rhythms of Local Church Collaboration

These combined four traits are hands-on expressions of the Father, who is *for us*, the Son, who is *with us*, and the Holy Spirit, who is *in us*. Churches who commit to these expressions, or rhythms, create spiritual bonds that look like our God.

So, let me boil that down into a single call to action that can guide our efforts:

> Create trinitarian collaborations by initiating relationships, building trust, celebrating diversity, and inviting inclusive voices into your fellowship.

Grab your spiritual headphones as we listen to each of these rhythms one at a time.

FIRST RHYTHM: RELATIONSHIP

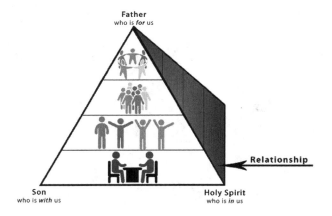

The foundational rhythm of collaboration is a relationship, which means "the way in which two or more people or things are connected or the state of being connected." It is also "the way in which two or more people or groups regard and behave towards each other."[1] I purposefully began this collaboration model with relationships because who we are in Christ prioritizes what we might do together.

Relationships require *affinity*. The connection we have with one another shapes effectiveness and sustainability for ministry partnerships. More important is that this model seeks to pattern itself after the triune God. The interconnection of the persons of the Trinity is undoubtedly a big deal. Remember Johnson's necessary conviction:

> "At the center of the universe is a relationship." That is the most fundamental truth I know. At the center of the universe is a community.[2]

Since it is a big deal to God, it should also be a big deal to his church. But first, we must grasp the importance of relationships.

1. Lexico, s.v. "Relationship," https://www.lexico.com/en/definition/relationship.

2. Johnson, *Experiencing the Trinity*, 37.

Interpersonal connections help collaborative efforts begin miles ahead of strangers that start with a shared cause. Without the foundation of solid relationships, a collaboration concludes soon after the project ends.

A critical question to ask would-be collaborators regarding relationships is this: "Am I willing to dedicate time and energy to building and nurturing our relationship?" In other words, "Do I feel an affinity with others in the group?" When collaboration mirrors the Trinity, relationships set the partnership in motion.

Here is a crucial principle: someone must initiate the relationship. My experience has taught me that establishing new kingdom friendships requires visionary leaders with high values for collaboration. These same leaders start community connections with city officials, nonprofit organizations, social workers, and a host of other resources capable of blessing their communities. Relationships will never form on their own without someone initiating them.

The Bottom Line

Collaboration built on "relationships" is solid and attractive. However, collaboration without a relationship is flighty and unsustainable for the gospel mission.

When considering local church collaboration, seek visionary leaders who want to know you better as fellow believers in Christ. There are shared affinities that should relationally connect you.

Examples include:

* gospel mission (sharing the redemptive news of Christ)

* love for your city (desiring your community to be a better place for everyone to live)

* protecting and caring for children's education, nutrition, safety, etc.

* feeding the poor

* standing for justice, defending the oppressed and abused

* pastoral heart (loving the people of your church)

A Warning

Relationships are *not* a means to an end! Genuine connections seed potential kingdom partnerships. Therefore, initiating friendships solely to do a joint project is disingenuous and counterproductive.

An Honest Question with an Honest Answer

Q. Is it possible to collaborate without initiating relationships?

A. Yes. But relationships strengthen collaboration for long-term, sustainable partnerships. Remember when Jesus prayed in Gethsemane, "My Father, if it be possible, let this cup pass from me; nevertheless, not as I will, but as you will" (Matt 26:39)? He uttered his raw, gut-wrenching prayer strengthened by his solid connection with the Father. Their eternal interdependence meant that he would not walk to Calvary alone. Likewise, believers ought never to walk alone on the *missio Dei*. Resist any urge to bypass relationships if you desire to be one.

SECOND RHYTHM: TRUST

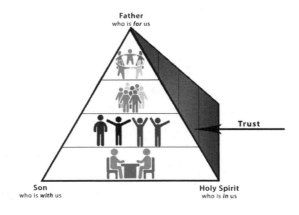

The second rhythm of collaboration is trust. It means "to believe that someone is good and honest and will not harm you, or that something is safe and reliable."[3] Trust needs *vulnerability*. It is the rhythm that flows out of consistent relationship narratives. Readers looking back on ministry partnerships will undoubtedly recall how their event was sweeter when the trust was present or how it soured when confidence was absent. Trust is necessary for congregations to create gospel beauty together. It should be the target outcome for collaboration built on relationships.

A critical question for churches and church leaders to ask regarding trust is this: "Am I willing to be personally and spiritually vulnerable with others?" In other words, "Do I rely on others in the group?" If so, the anticipated result of invested time and energy and nurturing of relationships will be trust dividends.

John Maxwell's executive leadership team recounts three questions that followers routinely ask their leaders: "Can you help me?" "Do you care about me?" "Can I trust you?"[4] Leaders should internalize these profound questions with four of their own: "How do I help them?" "How do I care for them?" "How do I build trust?" "How do we break trust?" Both sets of provocative questions confirm the importance of this model's second rhythm of collaboration.

Unfortunately, many partnerships function as task-oriented endeavors that overlook the critical need for relational trust. Their thinking might be that as long as the task ends favorably, the effort is a success. What derails such logic is when disagreements occur, miscommunication happens, or feelings get hurt. Suddenly the need for relational trust becomes glaringly apparent.

In difficult times, trustworthy leaders can "guide people through transition, conflict, and change. For the congregation to move forward, it needs to be able to trust the ability and heart of leadership—that the leaders are pursuing God's mission for the new ministry, looking out for people under their care, and

---

3. *Cambridge Dictionary*, s.v. "trust," https://dictionary.cambridge.org/us/dictionary/english/trust.

4. Holley and Goede, "Executive Leadership Podcast," para. 1.

providing direction and opportunities for their participation in the work of ministry."[5]

Here is a crucial principle: trust takes lots of time to develop, so prepare yourself for the long game. As one television chef always says, "Your patience will be rewarded."[6]

The Bottom Line

The more you trust a potential collaborator, the greater the chance you will collaborate with them. Building a history of consistent relational fellowship will ease your mind. You will sense over time that their word is their bond. Therefore, allow your trust to grow out of extended narratives together.

When partnering with other congregations, choose leaders that you trust. Then, when challenges or disagreements arise, you will weather those situations more effectively. Satan will use fear and mistrust to jeopardize your efforts to bless your cities. But trust mitigates fear over the issues that sabotage and destroy combined endeavors.

Examples of fear include:

* losing church members to a collaborating church

* pastor envy (members might prefer the collaborating pastor over you)

* usurping your autonomous identity (unity may become too influential in our decisions)

* theological/doctrinal differences ("nonessentials" may become tests of fellowship)

* pastor's job insecurity (collaboration might get you fired because it is not your job)

* mistrust over who is leading and who is in charge of the money

5. Chinn, *1 + 1 = 1*, 107.

6. "Your patience will be rewarded" is a famous quote from television chef Alton Brown ("Good Eats Quotes").

Warning

Trust *always* takes time! More profound confidence develops into practical and sustainable associations through the joyous and not-so-joyous times. The bitter seed of competition diminishes as well, leaving kingdom collaborators who are rooting for each other! Modeling the relational benefits of trust will undoubtedly encourage other believers to join your gospel movement.

An Honest Question with an Honest Answer

Q. Am I saying that church leaders have to be best friends to be effective collaborators?

A. No. Church leaders do not have to be best friends to be collaborators. Still, I am confident that leaders who effectively collaborate with relational trust often become good friends!

Churches and organizations partner all the time without a prior rhythm of trust. However, once their project or ministry concludes, often their fellowship ends too. Local congregations who are siloed and unfamiliar with one another join for good causes all the time. I am not dismissing their charitable work. However, this thesis advocates a type of partnership that grows from a foundation of relational trust. Leaders who are friends position their respective organizations to develop mutual rapport. In effect, their modeled friendship is contagious. Remember that the loving community of the triune God is our example for collaboration. Pray that would-be collaborators raise leaders whose relational trust mirrors the Trinity.

THIRD RHYTHM: DIVERSITY

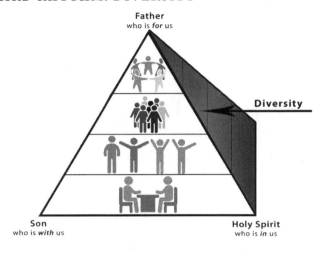

The third rhythm of collaboration is diversity, which describes "heterogeneity within a group on characteristics such as informational (professional background, education, skills), visible (race, age, ethnicity) or value-based (ethic, motivation) differences."[7] Remember how the Trinity is diverse. He is the Father, who is *for us*, the Son, who is *with us*, and the Holy Spirit, who is *in us*. Since the premise of this model is that local church collaboration is a practice of unity that mirrors the Trinity, our kingdom partnerships must also be diverse.

In fact, every community of faith consists of diverse people who are all God's image bearers. Therefore, their various skills, gifts, experiences, and personalities should inspire celebrations of God's creativity and artistry.

In addition to this, your city contains diverse local churches pursuing the *missio Dei*. Those "other" organizations/churches that are *so different* from "your" church have experiences, perspectives, insights, connections, knowledge, wisdom, etc. that *you* don't have.

Think about kingdom work like barbecuing Kansas City-style ribs. In this analogy, your church is a pair of hands, a nearby

7. Leander, "Diversity-Oriented Churches," para. 2.

church plant is a set of eyes, a larger church is a nose, and an older church comprises the taste buds. When you are doing tough stuff like kingdom collaboration, you *definitely* want hands and eyes and nose and taste buds working together to "Q" those ribs! Hands alone do not have what it takes by themselves. But together, you can produce mouthwatering ribs so tender that they fall off the bone. In the same way, diverse local churches mirror godlike unity whenever they celebrate their unique perspectives through complementary community actions. The more they collaborate, the better those ribs will turn out.

Isaiah prophesied about the diversity of the people of God:

> It shall come to pass in the latter days that the mountain of the house of the Lord shall be established as the highest of the mountains, and shall be lifted up above the hills; and all the nations shall flow to it, and many peoples shall come, and say: "Come, let us go up to the mountain of the Lord, to the house of the God of Jacob, that he may teach us his ways and that we may walk in his paths." For out of Zion shall go forth the law, and the word of the Lord from Jerusalem. (Isa 2:2–3)

See how "many people" flow to the mountainous house of the Lord from "all the nations." This illustrious rhythm is vital to every trinitarian ministry because it reflects God's design for his church. When we celebrate the diverse colors, ethnicities, spiritual gifts, and perspectives God placed into his church, we look more and more like him.

A critical question for churches and church leaders to ask regarding diversity is this: "Am I willing to be more intentional about celebrating and embracing our differences?" From a personal perspective: "Do I add uniqueness to the group?" Contrasting diversity to the first two elements, relationships require affinity and trust needs vulnerability. But diversity demands *intentional variety*. Relational trust is the suitable soil for variety to grow.

Here is a crucial principle: diversity already exists in your church, whether you recognize it or not. Expand your categories beyond race, color, and ethnicity to include education, socioeconomics, and season of life. You will quickly realize that your congregation has been diverse all along. Those precious souls are waiting for you to throw a party and celebrate them.

The Bottom Line

Work together with churches and organizations that are glaringly different than you. Fellowshipping with other believers is excellent practice for our future experience around the throne of glory. Listen to John's vision:

> After this I looked, and behold, a great multitude that no one could number, from every nation, from all tribes and peoples and languages, standing before the throne and before the Lamb, clothed in white robes, with palm branches in their hands, and crying out with a loud voice, "Salvation belongs to our God who sits on the throne, and to the Lamb!" (Rev 7:9–10)

God beautifully painted humanity with nuanced variety, textures, and complexity. Worshipers of God representing all tribes and peoples and languages will praise his name throughout eternity. As image bearers of the Holy One, our diversity will mirror him forever. So we might as well start practicing now!

To purposely practice diverse collaboration, look for churches that appear different to most casual observers.

Examples include:

* ethnicity (e.g., White church and Hispanic church)

* city location (rural church and inner-city church)

* sociodemographic (upper-middle-class church and middle-class church)

* denomination (Reformed church and UMC)

* worship style (piano/organ vs. full band)

* membership size (house church and large church)

A Warning

Diversity is *not* the goal! It is one step toward the goal. Do not be lulled into complacency. Praise God for all of the different types of people sitting around your church's ministry table. But remember that you have more work to do if you want to mirror the loving community of God. So do not stop; keep on going!

An Honest Question with an Honest Answer

Q. Can we not collaborate with churches similar to our church?

A. Yes. Church-affinity networks work together to accomplish great things all over the world. Homogenous churches pull resources together and distribute them daily to people in need. However, our world's multicultural coalition knows how powerfully compelling diversity is during this time in history. Diversity is culturally normative; everything else feels sectarian and odd. Recalling the barbecue analogy, more hands could assess the condition of the ribs to a point, but watchful eyes, a tuned-in nose, and a skilled taste palate will help those hands make the barbecue even better. More to the topic of this thesis, the three-and-one God of heaven sets the culture of his people. Our rich diversity follows the pattern of his relational nature. This project champions a unity culture that brings together Jesus followers who possess a broad spectrum of gifts and experiences. The world's multicultural coalition will notice our newly minted reputation—diverse people working together to offer hope to the nations.

FOURTH RHYTHM: INCLUSION

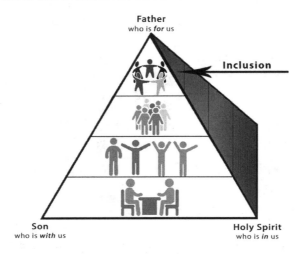

The fourth rhythm of trinitarian collaboration is inclusion, which describes "an organisational effort and practices in which different groups or individuals having different backgrounds are culturally and socially accepted and welcomed," and equally treated.[8] It is also "a sense of belonging. Inclusive cultures make people feel respected and valued for who they are as an individual or group. As a result, people feel a level of supportive energy and commitment from others so that they can do their best at work."[9]

Local church collaboration ignites potential when it engages the rhythm of inclusion. But it is essential to point out that diversity and inclusion are not the same rhythms. Often Christian leaders struggle to grasp their nuances. The way Dr. Paul Louis Metzger describes the difference is helpful: "Diversity is inviting different people to the dinner party. Inclusion is inviting everyone to help create the menu and make the meal."[10]

The labor equity needed to achieve diversity can be so taxing that leaders often make diversity the finale rather than the next

8. "What Is Diversity," para. 8.

9. "What Is Diversity," para. 10.

10. Paul Louis Metzger, email message to me, January 18, 2020.

step toward unity. DeYmaz provides excellent assistance on this subject by incorporating the theology of the mystery of the gospel into his case for diverse inclusion.

> In the 21st century, local church pastors seeking to position the church for effective community engagement, evangelism, discipleship, growth, health, development, and ultimately, measurable impact can no longer afford to proclaim the gospel of Jesus Christ apart from the gospel of Gentile inclusion.[11]

This type of *disruption,* meaning diverse believers inclusively living out the gospel in their cities, is a beautiful strategy to elevate the value of collaboration in the hearts and minds of Christian leaders.

If relationships require affinity, trust needs vulnerability, and diversity demands intentional variety, inclusion involves *humility.* The diverse beauty that grows out of relational trust sets the stage for inclusion.

A critical question for churches and church leaders to ask regarding inclusion is this: "Am I willing to listen more and talk less?" In other words, "Do I insist on hearing the unique voices in the group, and does the group insist on hearing my unique voice?" This idea is at the heart of inclusion—that is, "a sense of belonging. Inclusive cultures make people feel respected and valued for who they are as an individual or group. People feel a level of supportive energy and commitment from others."[12] Inclusion raises the bar of would-be collaboration because it mirrors the inclusive interdependence of the Father, Son, and Holy Spirit. The Trinity in action is a rhythmic dance of deference. We limit our gospel vision if ever we insist that our way is the only way.

Here is a crucial principle: visionary leaders must create a culture of invitation to galvanize other voices. These skilled leaders are phenomenal at transforming "my" plan into "our" plan. This notion may feel counterintuitive to your image of influential

---

11. DeYmaz, *Disruption*, 37.
12. "What Is Diversity," para. 10.

leaders. However, there is no such thing as an omniscient leader with perfect ideas. The truth is that every leader has blind spots—areas in which we would benefit from other's input.

For example, one of my dear friends and mentors had coffee with me in downtown Portland, Oregon. He told me lovingly but firmly, "Avery, you are always so hopeful. And that is a major blind spot for you!" I took a few minutes to ponder those words because I had never heard them before. Yet, he has known me and my quirky, artistic, always hopeful personality for fifteen years and counting. He already had my permission to speak into my life. So, I listened. Perhaps I am a better pastor and leader as a result of including his voice in my life.

To further illustrate why this rhythm is so crucial, let us imagine that your congregation has built a trusting relationship with a neighboring church. You agree to distribute care packages to homeless teens and offer physical and spiritual support. Your collaboration's effectiveness would benefit from the inclusion of voices like the following:

* a homeless teenager sharing their story and their needs

* a high school student suggesting ideas to reach and support their homeless classmates

* a laid-off engineer giving perspective on how some might respond to efforts of charity

* a recently employed single dad who has previously navigated the maze of government-assistance programs

* a resident who lives in a neighborhood where homeless people congregate

Every included voice would supply a frame of reference to benefit your kingdom initiative. Remember that the Father, Son, and Holy Spirit always invite one another to participate in their eternal work. This project's model unapologetically mimics their relational, inclusive community. They perfectly model this fourth rhythm of collaboration.

The Bottom Line

Inclusive leaders skillfully morph *their* ideas into *our* ideas for the sake of the gospel. Collaborative ideas benefit from diverse, inclusive partners working together. In other words, different people in the room produce diversity; different opinions from various people produce inclusion.

When considering local church collaboration, look for churches that insist that everyone involved contribute to the kingdom's success. Thus, the overused phrase is accurate: we are better together.

Examples where inclusion is needed:

* initial ideas (taking good pictures and making them a reality for a city)

* leadership teams

* support teams

* promotional material (visual and printed communication detailing the project)

* prayer covering (calling on the name of the Lord to bless kingdom efforts)

* worship events (multiple styles from multiple faith and ethnic traditions)

A Warning

Inclusion does *not* ignore or dismiss spiritual gifts and abilities! Instead, inclusion leverages those gifts and skills to nurture and benefit the collaboration. In other words, everyone sitting around the same meal table helps create the menu and prepare the meal. Praise God because *diverse inclusion anchored in relational trust* is the target for local church collaboration.

An Honest Question with an Honest Answer

Q. Does inclusion mean we must invite every church in our city to join our collaboration?

A. No. Every church will not collaborate with everyone, but I maintain that every church should collaborate with someone! Engage the four rhythms of collaboration to discover potential gospel connections prayerfully. Practice initiating relationships, building trust, and celebrating diversity. You will have the opportunity to invite inclusive voices into the strategy room. Then, through the power of the Holy Spirit, transform *your* idea into *their* idea to bless your city. It is more complex, takes more time, and involves more people. But the resulting collaboration will reflect the God of heaven and earth!

BEFORE WE MOVE ON . . .

At this point, some of you are rolling your eyes. No doubt you have questions and concerns or flat out disagree with me. Regardless, I implore you to center those reactions on the heart of Christ. We must get past our platitudes of unity and commit to practicing it daily. Every decision your church makes either moves us toward harmony in Christ or away from it. I suggest that these four rhythms can help move us toward unity.

Let me help you visualize what I am describing with a personal story.

THE MILLION-DOLLAR TABLE

Picture a White dude drinking coffee with a slightly older Black dude at a sidewalk-café table in a quirky Silicon Valley downtown. Now add business stiffs wheeling and dealing, groups of techie types eating lunch, older people talking loudly about whatever, younger people hunting down their favorite caffeine fix, and a bunch of hurried pedestrians late to who knows where. Next, insert a salesman pitching the brand-new Tesla parked in front of the café and a mom's group happy to be around adults for a change. Imagine limited available parking on a bustling street. Inhale the aromas of scratch-made Italian cuisine from the restaurant on the left, freshly seasoned Middle Eastern cuisine from the restaurant on the right, and freshly baked goods from the bakery across the street, with the stimulating bouquet of freshly brewed coffee from inside the quirky coffee shop. Visualize blue skies with perfect weather year-round. This setting was Murphy Avenue, where I got to know my brother Dan.

He grew up in the Bay Area, where tech is king. I grew up in the San Joaquin Valley, where agriculture rules.

He ran his own nonprofit company in the wellness industry. I was a staff pastor for the church we both attended.

He was tall, good-looking, and physically fit. I was the guy who was not so tall and needed to get into shape.

He spoke Gen X fluently with a millennial accent. I spoke Gen X fluently with a ghetto accent.

He found the Lord later in life than me. I led my first worship song when I was two years old.

Every week, two very different guys sat at that sidewalk table drinking coffee and talking about whatever. We never had a business meeting, a counseling session, or a bait-and-switch appointment with an ulterior motive. We just drank coffee and talked. No topics were ever out of bounds. Imposed judgments were never guests at the table. Sometimes we sat in silent grief over a loss or a disappointment. Other times we would freak people out by praising Jesus—loudly! Now and then, we vetted crazy kingdom dreams. But the power of that table was that two men with very little in common intentionally scheduled time to meet out in the public square for everyone to witness.

One afternoon, an enthusiastic stranger interrupted our conversation like an overly zealous five-year-old who just won the Christmas-gift lottery at grandma's house. He loudly commented on how amazing the weather was and how blessed we were to sit at such a "million-dollar table" at a sidewalk café. As he walked away,

Dan and I looked at one another as if a light bulb had simultaneously turned on in our brains. In that instance, the Million-Dollar Table was born. $TAB became our texting shorthand to schedule time on Murphy Avenue. Sometimes, life was so tough that we sat quietly without talking much. We could share pain, victories, failures, family struggles, ministry angst, or none of the above. As it turns out, $TAB was a protected and safe table to initiate relationships, build trust, celebrate diversity, and invite inclusion.

At the time, I was clueless.

A Contagious Table

Ministry ideas either started or sharpened at the Million-Dollar Table, creating a contagious vibe. One such idea was a sermon series about revival. Our pastor Joel had asked me to lead a five-week series that summer, so I chose revival as the topic. My idea for the series was a lecture-lab model: preach about revival (whatever *that* is) on Sunday morning and lead Sunday-evening practicums to experience what we learned that morning. I will never forget Dan's reaction when he heard my idea. He paused (way too long) before asking a lovingly blunt question: "Revival? What is *that*?" By the time we left $TAB several hours later, I had a reframed idea for the series on revival called *Reignition*. Days later, I was standing at a whiteboard in a room filled with gifted people wanting to help. Soon after, stage designers, worship leaders, Bible teachers, party managers, graphic artists, and others from our church began offering their ideas to produce the transformative series *Reignition*. Our collaborative fire caught on and (hopefully) blessed others that summer.

And It Keeps Going and Going

Many years later, every ministry I lead or church collaboration I participate in starts by nurturing a relational foundation. One example is the Mosaix PDX Network led by my brother Dave. He and

I met several years ago for a casual chat at a coffeehouse. When 2020's racial dissonance escalated, Dave (who is White) invited me to join two other Black pastors to lead Mosaix PDX in a single conversation about the Black experience. That session turned into thirteen conversations over thirteen consecutive months. Participants from multiple churches were predominantly White believers committed to learning, repenting, lamenting, and growing together in Christ.

But the wave did not stop there.

Pastor Cliff, Pastor Levell, and I (the three Black pastors) met for coffee about a year ago. We have grown together in Christ during our collaborative experience with Mosaix PDX. Each of us comes from different backgrounds and experiences. But we built enough relational cache for them to invite me to join Portland's newly minted Coalition of African/African American Pastors (CAAAP). This group of leaders is a powerhouse of spiritual wisdom, gifts, and decades of missional work historically embedded in the city's DNA. It is my honor to know these great men of God.

But wait, there's more.

The Equity Committee from Oregon Health and Science University Hospital (OHSU) contacted CAAAP with aspirations of convincing Black pastors to host COVID-19 vaccination clinics at our church facilities. They hoped that the trust we built over time in our community would engender confidence among ethnic residents with historically-based trust issues.[13] A meeting between equity team members and CAAAP members led to

13. Two ethnic communities in particular are hesitant to receive COVID-19 vaccinations, and for good reasons. African Americans remember the gruesome atrocity of the 1932 "Tuskegee Study of Untreated Syphilis in the Negro Male." This one event is so incorporated into Black history that it often evokes automatic mistrust for any medical injections ("Tuskegee Timeline"). Latinos statistically feel more favorable about receiving the vaccine, according to US News & World Report. Among the obstacles preventing vaccinations, the fear of deportation for undocumented residents is real. I spoke with one OHSU doctor specifically about this issue. He emphatically said that they do not care about citizen status. All they want is to help prevent people from contracting or spreading COVID-19. Yet, the mistrust in these communities remain as obstacles ("Hispanics Eager").

Common Ground hosting two Pfizer clinics in central Beaverton, collaborating with four other local congregations. Our first clinic administered 124 first-shot doses; the second administered first and second doses totaling 134 shots.

I could go on and tell you about our new collaboration with Pastor Ed and Mt. Olivet Church in Aloha or our upcoming partnership with social workers from a neighboring high school. But the point is to demonstrate how waves of collaboration can begin with one conversation over a cup of coffee. Imagine the collaborative work you and your church can accomplish if you initiate a similarly contagious table.

FIVE OBSERVATIONS FROM THE MILLION-DOLLAR TABLE

What made $TAB such a life-changing force in my life? Let me share a quick flow of five observations.

First, conversations were relational without side agendas. As my grandmother would say, we never "put on airs." The relationship itself was the plan. Friendship was the sole motivation. Try not to overthink this. Dan and I hung out together to hang out together—and to drink coffee!

Second, we built a ton of trust over four years. $TAB strengthened our friendship, which helped when we saw life or ministry differently. Make no mistake about it—relational credibility requires time, and there are never any shortcuts.

Third, our differences brought a dynamic vitality to the Million-Dollar Table. Most of the time, I learned way more than I ever taught. The more our trust grew, the more I felt I could be myself, not compromise my values, soften my blackness, or squash my passion for ministry.

Fourth, we were insistent about hearing the other guy's perspective and receiving his contribution to a formulating idea. Yes, it was also an excuse for good coffee! But much more than that, $TAB was more about listening than it ever was about talking.

Murphy Avenue rounds out my observations. Simply put, the Million-Dollar Table was in the marketplace, where crowds could casually or critically watch. People constantly asked why we were meeting, which gave us an excuse to put the love of Jesus on blast!

YOUR PASTORS NEED TO DRINK MORE COFFEE!

I know a lot of pastors, and most of them do not have very many friends.

Some of them do not have any friends.

The majority of their connections are business relationships. Interactions are mainly in conjunction with their pastoral roles. Seldom do they have margin in their packed schedules to initiate non-ministry-related friendships. Even at casual gatherings, people usually ask pastors to pray over the food. After all, why else would you invite a pastor to your party?

Imagine how seemingly absurd it would be if a pastor scheduled ten hours in the workweek solely to hang out with friends. Church leaders might react negatively, saying, "The pastor is out doing *what* on ministry time? They can spend time with friends on their *own* time!" That comment would typify the expectations that many church leaders have for their staff employees.

Let me dig deeper into that reality. If authentic relationships are rare in your church, it might be because your pastor is modeling string-attached relationships. Worship centers can fill up every weekend with strangers who happen to attend the same church. That level of spiritual connection flies out the window when crisis hits or conflict arises—or when the same video shows up on all of their newsfeeds. You will want sustained relationships through the toughest of times. Your pastor needs permission to initiate real friendships, the foundation for mirroring the Trinity—and it needs to be paid time on the clock!

Leaders, if you want your church to thrive, encourage your pastors to drink more coffee.

Decaf is occasionally acceptable!

SUMMARY OF THE FOUR RHYTHMS OF TRINITARIAN COLLABORATION

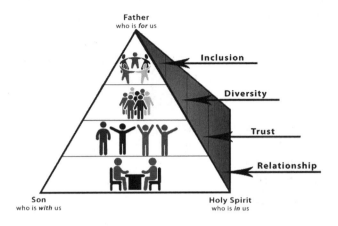

Any leader or organization that wants their partnerships to be effective and thrive with longevity should incorporate these actions. Make them more than procedures; embed them into your culture.

Four Rhythms	Relationships	Trust	Diversity	Inclusion
Require(s):	affinity	vulnerability	intentional variety	humility
Crucial Principle:	someone must initiate the relationship	trust takes lots of time to develop, so prepare for the long game	diversity already exists in your church—you just need the eyes to recognize it	visionary leaders must create a culture of invitation to galvanize other voices
Action Step:	initiate relationships, not just service projects	build relational trust, not just your church brand	celebrate diversity, not just your church history	invite inclusive voices, not just visitors, to attend your church

DEVOTIONAL REFLECTIONS
(INDIVIDUALLY OR IN SMALL GROUPS)

1. Read 1 John 3:1–3, Isa 53:1–5, and John 16:12–15. Use your favorite translation plus a paraphrase like The Passion Translation. Focus on the ways the Father, Son, and Holy Spirit demonstrate their love for you. Spend ten to fifteen minutes highlighting your Bible or writing them down.

2. Consider how the Father, Son, and Holy Spirit model the four rhythms. Then write down ways that you and your church can model him (in small groups, share your insights).

3. Pray over the four rhythms of collaboration (initiate relationships, build trust, celebrate diversity, invite inclusion). Then, write down a few ways you and your church can jump into the flow (in small groups, share your insights).

4. Take a few minutes and imagine your city filled with churches that flow in these rhythms. Then, write down what comes to mind (in small groups, share your dreams, concerns, etc.).

5. Prayer focus: "Holy Trinity, empower your children to be a public display of heaven on earth."

6. Song of reflection: "O Praise the Name" as performed by This Hope.

TWO PRAYERS

Father God, in the name of Jesus,

As he lifted up his voice to you in John 17, declaring, "the glory which thou gavest me I have given them; that they may be one, even as we are one" (John 17:22 KJV).

It is my prayer that this glory rest upon the body of Christ in this dispensation of time. We shall become a house of prayer for all people, as God has declared it to be so through the prophet Isaiah.

Restore the glory that powers our witness to be undeniable on the earth.

Father God, in the name of Jesus, we declare a shaking and a breaking down of the strongholds of racism/prejudice that have held the church back over one hundred years from being the people you have preordained us to be. Repair the breach that Lucifer has caused through his doctrine of division.

We are demolishing arguments, ideas, and every high-and-mighty philosophy that pits itself against the knowledge of the one true God. We are taking prisoners of every thought, every emotion, and subduing them into obedience to the Anointed One.

We believe that all things are possible if we have your glory that comes by our unity. Communities will be healed, souls will be saved, and revival will come. It shall be done in Jesus' name!

Apostle Levell Thomas
Oasis of Praise International Ministries
Portland, Oregon

Father God,

It is my prayer that the commanded blessing of Ps 133 rest upon the body of Christ. We know this can only happen as we dwell together in unity. May the heart of your children yearn for the unity of the faith. Let the light of our oneness shine bright and dispel all the divisive forces of darkness that war against our testimony in the earth.

Let your anointing create a dwelling of unity among your chosen people that destroys the yoke of separatism and isolation. Grace us with oneness of mind, oneness of voice, and singleness of heart that glorifies you.

Pastor Mark Jackson, Co-laborer
Oasis of Praise International Ministries
Portland, Oregon

Chapter 6

Essentials and Hurdles

Tells the musician how loud or soft notes should be played.

—Dynamics (dynamic marking)

When it comes to gospel partnerships, theology and practice collide at the point of human individuality. As a result, some collabs seem destined for success while others fracture for various reasons. Admittedly, the four rhythms of collaboration paint a copacetic picture for practicing unity. So, let me acknowledge what is obvious—implementing this model will not be easy. The spiritual investment necessary for impactful kingdom partnerships requires prayerful interaction with diversely gifted people. The process is a fruitful one, but it is hard work.

Here is where I want you to hit the brakes on using this model as your next trending church program. That would be insanity. We do not need more programs; what we need is a new culture for the twenty-first-century church.

Did I mention that this will be hard work?

COLLABORATION VS. COLLABORATION CULTURE

The idea of culture means "the way of life, especially the general customs and beliefs, of a particular group of people at a particular time."[1] I want to be clear on this topic—this model of collaboration is not an optional program for local congregations to adopt or reject. It is an intentional new normal for the body of Christ.

One project-management company in Australia, Atlassian, recognizes the difference between collaboration and establishing a collaborative culture:

> A collaborative culture is one where collaboration is regular and deliberate. Collaboration doesn't just occur if someone happens to initiate it. Instead, it's baked into processes of how people do their work every day and into the attitudes they take about that work. At its heart, a collaborative culture values the idea that we are better together.[2]

Similarly, local church collaboration that mirrors the Trinity should be the cadence of daily life for the twenty-first-century church. I maintain that Jesus' desire for us to be one was more than a temporary event with a start and end date. He was praying that our loving unity would become our regular and deliberate lifestyle.

OUR PIVOTAL DECISION

In the summer of 2017, Common Ground Church (multiracial, predominantly Asian American), where I currently serve on staff, searched for available facilities to rent for Sunday gatherings and midweek ministries. Our search led to a church campus in Beaverton with six autonomous congregations meeting on their campus. Their ethnicities included two White congregations, one Chinese, one Korean, one Latino, and one Bhutanese. Initially, the new

1. *Cambridge Dictionary*, s.v. "culture," https://dictionary.cambridge.org/us/dictionary/english/culture.

2. "How to Create," para. 8–9.

pastor of the host church was uninterested in renting more space. But after viewing our website and hearing my heart for collaboration (not just cohabitation), he invited Common Ground (CG) to join their campus in the late summer. As it turns out, his value for partnerships was similar to mine. That decision was pivotal for the creation of this project.

Since then, CG has built varying degrees of relationships with the campus churches. But honestly, I assumed that collaboration would be easy. How simpler could combined efforts get than multiple congregations worshiping on the same campus? I had a lot more to learn about how leaders are shaped and gifted by Christ. My learning process became the two-year-long case study for my doctoral thesis.

For the rest of this chapter, I will share six essentials to building a collaborative culture and six hurdles that threaten it. In no way do they comprise an exhaustive list, but these essentials and hurdles represent lessons learned during my case study. Advance awareness of these insights can prepare you for the hard work ahead. Remember that our objective for collaboration is to mirror the loving community of the Father, Son, and the Holy Spirit. Let me break that down again:

> Like the Father, who is *for us*, believers must *root for one another*.

> Like the Son, who is *with us*, we must commit to *being with one another*.

> Like the Holy Spirit, who is *in us*, Jesus' followers must *keep one another in our hearts*.

So, roll up your sleeves and let us count the cost of sitting at the same banquet table. It can be the most fulfilling work of your life.

SIX ESSENTIALS TO BUILDING COLLABORATION CULTURE

The first three essentials are somewhat unique to kingdom partnerships. However, the last three essentials apply to any kingdom effort and become *even more* critical for collaborations.

A SOLID THEOLOGY (THE FIRST ESSENTIAL)

Ministry vision apart from theology is dangerous because human wisdom shapes it rather than God's design. How much more will a culture change require solid biblical theology? Chapter 2 lays out my theology for collaboration to teach and inspire Christian leaders to take the practice of oneness more seriously. Otherwise, Jesus' prayer in John 17 will remain wishful thinking for churches to dismiss and continue their habits of siloed isolation. When you can embrace a biblical theology that connects our oneness with our gospel effectiveness, you will be on your way to building new rhythms of collaboration in your church.

A VARIETY OF LEADERS (THE SECOND ESSENTIAL)

Pastors tend to view collaboration as superfluous to their ministry job description. Why? Where does the dissonance between spiritual roles and ministry jobs originate? One of my discoveries with our campus churches is that pastors can be influential without being visionary leaders. Mike Breen and Scott Cockram speak to this point in their discussion about the five ministries of Eph 4:11–13, which include apostles, prophets, evangelists, pastors, and teachers.[3] The writers comment:

> The fivefold ministries in Ephesians 4 are for "each one of us." ". . . grace has been given as Christ apportioned it." The fivefold roles apply to all members of the body of

3. Breen and Cockram, *Discipling Culture*, 101–4.

Christ in varying degrees. What Paul is saying is that Jesus, by the gift of his grace, has empowered and equipped each of us for service. We have all been given different-sized portions of grace and anointing. We each receive part of the whole. Christ's ministry fully demonstrates all five roles of apostle, prophet, evangelist, pastor, and teacher. We, as members in his body, receive one of these five appointments, relying on one another for those areas we are not gifted in.[4]

Since all these roles represent the fullness of Christ, local congregations need all five ministries to be the body of Christ. Breen and Cockram categorize these roles into two categories: Pioneers (apostolic, prophetic, and evangelistic) and Settlers (pastoral and teaching).[5]

Visionaries and Pragmatists

Pioneers "enjoy change and find the stress of doing new things exciting rather than threatening."[6] Settlers are "committed to continuity, stability, and conservation. They prefer to grow and develop plans rather than scrap what they have and start over with something brand new."[7] Both pioneers (visionaries) and settlers (pragmatists) are necessary for the functioning of local churches.

Here is where the lightbulb turned on for me—

Most pastors are settlers, *not* visionaries.

Though pastors have the most influential leadership role in most churches, their primary, often exclusive, jobs (and passions) include feeding, protecting, and caring for their flock. Those are qualities of shepherds, one of the pragmatic roles.

Eureka!

I have always assumed that all pastors were visionaries. I was wrong.

4. Breen and Cockram, *Discipling Culture*, 99.

5. Breen and Cockram, *Discipling Culture*, 109.

6. Breen and Cockram, *Discipling Culture*, 108.

7. Breen and Cockram, *Discipling Culture*, 109.

Pastors are seldom the loudest voices promoting crazy ideas like collaboration, unity, city-wide campaigns for Christ, compassion networks, racial reconciliation, and so on. Instead, the visionary roles (apostolic, prophetic, and evangelistic) usually engage in such crazy talk.

During my case-study years, I tried to convince God-appointed pastors to join CG in pioneering efforts, namely collaboration. Yet God's calling in *their* lives was to be passionate shepherds. They keep their sheep together in a common fold and call them out by name to go to pasture (John 10). And they are faithful stewards of their spiritual roles.

So, what is the solution that would point us toward normative collaboration?

Get Everyone in the Room Where It Happens

Collaboration culture requires *both* visionaries and pragmatists to lean together into the heart of unity. Otherwise, well-intentioned pragmatists will continually block pioneering ideas, and well-meaning visionaries will constantly accuse settlers of being small-minded and unrighteous. The key to elevating the value of collaboration is to get all five roles in the same room and humbly initiate relationships, build trust, celebrate diversity, and invite inclusion.

A Caution to Avoid Tokenism

Churches can excel at nondiscriminatory hiring policies but fail at intentionally embracing differences. We have all seen the church staff photos that ooze smiles, youthful energy, different skin colors, and multigenerational acceptance. But, buyer, beware: church website photos can mask some well-intentioned tokenism.

Cook defines tokenism as "the superficial inclusion of underrepresented groups as an attempt to dodge criticism for the organizational omission of diversity."[8] Leadership teams who want to fix their lack of visionaries or pragmatists can also fall into this trap. Manufacturing church diversity, as a general rule, is the wrong way to go. Tokenism compounds the dysfunction with the illusion that everyone at the table will decide on the menu and cook the food. However, the reality is that the same ol' meatloaf dinner will remain the only entrée. The chefs just needed a colorful team around the dinner table to smile for the Instagram shot.

Alternatively, local churches should intentionally gather gifted people to invite their diverse voices to contribute to the gospel mission. Do not push decisions to look diverse; make your decisions to be one! If that is your intent, then you are on a quest to be like our triune God. That is a worthwhile pursuit.

A HIGH VALUE FOR COLLABORATION (THE THIRD ESSENTIAL)

Look at any pastoral job description, and you can quickly tell whether collaboration is valued or not. Except to support an occasional evangelist or Christian artist coming into town, church leaders tend to keep to themselves and seldom venture outside their clan territory. I acknowledge that my background is unique. Kingdom collaboration is essential to me because of my spiritual heritage and past and current ministry contexts. What about your background? How does it elevate or deflate your value for practicing unity? Perhaps your experience has been ministering exclusively in your congregation or your church denomination. Maybe you have partnered with area pastors but the negative experience soured the idea. Perhaps you collaborate only within your ethnic church network. Maybe you have never developed a biblical theology that gave you a burning desire to partner with other local churches. Whatever your experience may be, it contributes to or repels you from the practice of oneness in Christ. Bottom line: we will not give our lives to something that we do not value.

8. Cook, "Gift of Going Second," para. 11.

A CLEAR DEFINITION AND VISION
(THE FOURTH ESSENTIAL)

Clearly defined vision is a universal prerogative for any effort—without a clear objective to drive toward, the chance of success goes way down. If we are unsure which target to zero in on, how will we know if we hit the mark? This dynamic becomes even more critical in the crucible of diverse multiparty relationships. I noticed early on in this project that the campus pastors lacked objective metrics for collaborative success. As a result, they resisted promoting one another's efforts, unsure how cross-promotions could benefit (or hinder) their congregation. Opaque vision laced with vague descriptors like "partners" can be met with comments like:

> Why do *we* have to take money out of *our* general fund to help *them* with *their* idea?

> What if some of *our* members start liking *their* church better than *ours*?

> Why do *we* have to go to *that* side of town?

> Why do *we* always have to go to *their* church, and *they* never come to *our* church?

I know the frustration of leaving a planning meeting with more questions than answers.

> Are we leading together, am I following your lead, or are we in need of a leader?

> Is there a designated idea, or are we creating something new together?

> Is this a "one-off" project, or do you need me to attend all the meetings?

> Is "partnership" actually code for "I need your money and volunteers"?

These kinds of questions suggest that visionary leaders are sometimes unclear when proposing collaboration to potential kingdom partners. Terms and definitions ought never to be ambiguous.

Dave Raymond offers ten definitions, or models, for collaboration.[9] For example, merging two or more churches is different than one church absorbing or adopting another church. This project will argue that the desired end state of that collaboration largely shapes the definition of collaboration. Are these steps toward a church merger, a partnership to meet community needs through specific ministries, or something else? Congregational and pastoral collaborations should never be uncomfortably vague for prospective participants. Butler agrees that defining the parameters for churches "working together" is essential.[10] Remember, the objective is to reach cities for Christ together.

A KINGDOM MINDSET (THE FIFTH ESSENTIAL)

Churches often view one another as rivals, not partners. Remember from chapter 4 how union and unity are not the same? Though my case study involved seven churches on the same campus, that did not automatically make them kingdom partners. *Rooting for Rivals* affirms that the clan mentality is pervasive among churches and is a big problem. It is more than a problem; it is a nonstarter for gospel conversations in a twenty-first-century world that is increasingly aware of and disillusioned by the judgmental and hateful aspects of the Christian church's history. When the world begins to attribute unity and love to the people of God, the church will gain relational influence to speak hope into their lives. Butler agrees again and writes, "The credibility of our message is strengthened. Jesus says that those watching our lives and work are more likely to believe that he is who he says he is when they observe us working together. This is particularly true in the traditional, community-based cultures of Asia, Africa, and Latin America."[11] The unity of

9. Raymond, "Churches Can Work Together."

10. Butler, *Well Connected*, 273.

11. Butler, *Well Connected*, 30.

believers, the expressed heart of Christ (John 17:11, 20–23), is the path that leads us to the hearts of our friends and neighbors (John 13:34–35).

This project's model of collaboration views any church's success as every church's success! Greer, Horst, and Heisey's experience in the nonprofit arena helped reshape their metrics for success. Like Steve Jobs, they rejected the idea that other nonprofit organizations had to lose so that their nonprofit could win. They stopped measuring success by comparing their organization to their so-called rivals:

> Nothing crushes collaboration and friendship faster than comparison. . . . There are two extremes: we either begin to believe that our organization is superior because our numbers look better, or we are crushed, by comparison, becoming disheartened by the relative success of another organization. Competition inhibits a giving spirit. Why would we want to share with others when we measure our success against theirs? It is a mindset that leads to insularity, trade secrets, and closed fists instead of open hands.[12]

Adding to this point, the authors cite a lecture by Ajith Fernando, author and teaching director at Youth for Christ in Sri Lanka, who lamented the secularist nature of clannism in God's church and offered staunch warnings in his lecture. "Very soon we will find it difficult to sustain the metaphor of the body of Christ," Fernando said. "We believe in a lot of bodies of Christ . . . [but] there is one body of Christ."[13] What if we believed, like Fernando, that there simply are no competing teams within the body of Christ? As Greer, Horst, and Heisey argue, "Embracing this worldview would make our witness, our friendships, and our impact exceedingly greater."[14]

---

12. Greer et al., *Rooting for Rivals*, 160.
13. Fernando, "Way of Unifying Passion."
14. Greer et al., *Rooting for Rivals*, 38.

AN ATMOSPHERE OF PRAYER
(THE SIXTH ESSENTIAL)

In my estimation, our campus pastors never prioritized building friendships or regularly praying with and for one another. We seldom shared personal prayer requests. This missed opportunity was disappointing, since praying for one another contributes to the growth of kingdom partnerships. It is my experience that the more pastors pray for each other, the more they grow together in fellowship. Some "acts of love" are hindered by time commitments and other constraints, but prayer is a spiritual discipline that everybody can do. It could further bind us through times of joy and pain. We needed improvement in this area.

My passion for seeing God's people in perfect harmony began with one prayer (John 17). Since Jesus thought it essential to communicate his heart to the Father, we should do the same.

Prayer beautifully connects believers to God with his permission, which is why the apostle Paul was an advocate for prayer.

> Rejoice always, pray without ceasing, give thanks in all circumstances; for this is the will of God in Christ Jesus for you. (1 Thess 5:16–18)

> Do not be anxious about anything, but in everything by prayer and supplication with thanksgiving let your requests be made known to God. (Phil 4:6)

> And this is the confidence that we have toward him, that if we ask anything according to his will, he hears us. And if we know that he hears us in whatever we ask, we know that we have the requests that we have asked of him. (1 John 5:14–15)

Remember that the practice of unity is not simply a program but a church culture change. Local churches will never achieve this without God's help; neither will well-intentioned parachurch organizations produce unity events without God's help. Their attempts at verisimilitude seem always to fall short of the unity goal, leaving hopeful participants with a future of siloed "business as usual." We need the Spirit's continual heart stirring for the hard work ahead. Our prayer connection with God keeps us close to him while striving to be close to one another.

> I, therefore, a prisoner for the Lord, urge you to walk in a manner worthy of the calling to which you have been called, with all humility and gentleness, with patience, bearing with one another in love, eager to maintain the unity of the Spirit in the bond of peace. (Eph 4:1–3)

> Only let your manner of life be worthy of the gospel of Christ, so that whether I come and see you or am absent, I may hear of you that you are standing firm in one spirit, with one mind striving side by side for the faith of the gospel. (Phil 1:27)

Consider the difficulty of diverse personalities, passions, ethnicities, experiences, styles, forms of brokenness, etc. all walking in step with one another for the sake of the gospel. Without a prayerful atmosphere where the Spirit reigns, wannabe partnerships are at the mercy of subjective opinions and preferences. Most leaders abandon their efforts because the stress is not worth the hassle. But prayer takes the steam out of our emotions and refocuses us on seeking peace and harmony together.

> Put on then, as God's chosen ones, holy and beloved, compassionate hearts, kindness, humility, meekness, and patience, bearing with one another and, if one has a complaint against another, forgiving each other; as the Lord has forgiven you, so you also must forgive. And above all these, put on love, which binds everything together in perfect harmony. And let the peace of Christ rule in your hearts, to which indeed you were called in one body. And be thankful. (Col 3:12–15)

No collaboration plan is as power inducing as believers calling on the name of the Lord. Uniquely, prayer is our request *to collaborate with* the Father, the Son, and the Holy Spirit. Think about that for a while, then commit to this trinitarian prayer: "Holy Father, help your children be one by the power of your Spirit. In Jesus' name, amen!"

SIX HURDLES THAT THREATEN COLLABORATION CULTURE: THE POWER DIVIDE (THE FIRST HURDLE)

The first hurdle involves power. All partnerships have power dynamics to navigate. The nuances vary from case to case, but the underlying reality is relatively straightforward. People constitute a continuum of power. In a contrasting world of big and small, poor and rich, superior and subordinate, educated and more educated, it is hard work getting diverse churches to partner together. Take something as low-key as congregations worshiping together or spring-cleaning the campus of a neighborhood school. How complicated could those simple events be?

Very complicated!

Let me describe one example from my ministry experience that demonstrates power dynamics.

The Owner-Tenant Relationship

A challenging power dynamic exists within the owner-tenant relationship. For example, churches that own property may choose to rent space to other congregations. Even if a tenant congregation is a driving force behind some collaboration opportunities, they will always feel insecure in this scenario because they do not have an owner's stake in the building or property. As a result, they can be evicted from the campus at any time and for any reason. Common Ground knows this feeling very well; we have never owned a building in our fifteen-year history.

Tenants pay rent, and owners determine rental fees. Further, the renters must ask the owners for permission to schedule rooms, use equipment, change décor, calendar events, receive mail at the building, etc. Owners can grant or deny all requests.

When the owners summon the tenants to meetings, the lessees are often contractually obligated to attend. Thus, the saying "My house, my rules!" is their reality and a significant hurdle for developing a genuinely trusting relationship.

Unintentionally or not, churches with an owner-tenant relationship have an undeniable power dynamic—while professing to be one.

Space Sharing is a Popular Model

It is no secret that churches everywhere are struggling. A recent report stated the following:

> 6 in 10 Protestant churches are plateaued or declining in attendance and more than half saw fewer than 10 people become new Christians . . . . Three in 5 (61 percent) [of] pastors say their churches faced a decline in worship attendance or growth of 5 percent or less in the last three years. Almost half (46 percent) say their giving decreased or stayed the same from 2017 to 2018. More than 2 in 5 churches (44 percent) only have one or fewer full-time staff members. Close to 9 in 10 pastors (87 percent) say their church had the same or fewer number of full-time staff in 2018 as they had in 2017, including 7 percent who cut staff.[15]

As a result of declining memberships and finances, some pastors consider leasing church facilities to other churches as part of a larger vision for collaboration. However, when their relationship begins out of fiscal or organizational need rather than gospel conviction, an uncomfortable power dynamic will usually persist. Their contract produces an awkward business vibe disguised as a ministry partnership. It is inevitable. Owners default to the role of landlords for their campus tenants—and in the body of Christ, there is only room for one Lord!

My intent is not to condemn the space-sharing model. On the contrary, owners who allow other congregations to use their facilities are gracious and show commendable generosity. I am, however, suggesting that the four rhythms of collaboration can navigate power dynamics like the owner-tenant relationship. Tenants come

---

15. Earls, "Small, Struggling Congregations," para. 2, 5–6.

and go—but relationships, trust, diversity, and inclusion can turn owners and tenants into kingdom partners.

THE PRIVILEGE DIVIDE (THE SECOND HURDLE)

The second hurdle to overcome for kingdom collaboration involves privilege. I maintain that White believers waste too much time denying and dismissing their privilege when they ought to embrace it and leverage it to lift distant others and speak on behalf of the voiceless. Mark DeYmaz believes similarly regarding White guilt:

> Individually, it's not about guilt. Collectively, however, it's about those of us who have been born White men in America taking the time to understand and lament historical inequities and, like Christ, leveraging any measure of power and privilege we have today not for ourselves but for the sake of others.[16]

James Davison Hunter's theological reflections on rethinking power note the shortsighted neo-Anabaptist view that "the mark of true discipleship is to 'accept powerlessness.'"[17] In reality, "the church and its faithful are implicated in nearly every way in the exercise, exchange, and contest of power."[18] Hunter offers a theological way forward: "To be made in the image of God and to be charged with the task of working in and cultivating, preserving, and protecting the creation, is to possess power. The creation mandate, then, is a mandate to use that power in the world in ways that reflect God's intentions."[19] Possessing power is not innately evil. However, what is terrible and unfortunate is when believers use their power, prestige, status, and privilege to lift themselves rather than lift others and show them the saving grace of the cross.

---

16. DeYmaz, *Disruption*, 174.

17. Hunter, *To Change the World*, 181.

18. Hunter, *To Change the World*, 181.

19. Hunter, *To Change the World*, 183.

Some hurdles are more complicated to overcome than others, but they will never be slain by pretending they do not exist. Unfortunately, one example is a racially charged land mine.

The White Church-Ethnic Church Relationship

Church leaders interpret unity in Christ through the lens of our racially divided world. As a result, ethnic leaders can view their White counterparts as superior rather than equal.

Here is what I mean—

Dad passed on a saying about race that he learned growing up in rural Oklahoma. The saying was this: "If you're White, you're right. If you're Brown, you can stick around. But if you're Black, you better get in the back!" I cite this saying because many people of color have internalized it. The result is a nagging feeling that somehow we are *less than* White people.

People of color understand the worldview that Whiteness is always better than the rest. How? We learned this by living in America underneath non-white skin. Cultural Whiteness, especially in the West, is accepted as the gold standard for everything. So it is in our church culture. The best music, best sermons, greatest evangelists, best promotional materials, best neighborhoods to plant churches, best conferences to attend, etc. are supposedly all White.

This cultural philosophy is why some ethnic pastors view their White counterparts as superior—everything White is always better.

Unfortunately, this has caused ethnic people to internalize this message and believe we are less. This view directly affects how diverse pastors endeavor to build equitable relationships.

Over the tenure of my pastoral ministry, I watched ethnic church leaders cower and let go of their prayerful ideas for no other reason than that their White counterparts objected. Several White pastors and I have discussed this issue on many occasions, but some have yet to understand their cultural position of privilege fully. To the point of this discussion, ethnic pastors would benefit from hearing their White brothers affirm our oneness in Christ rather than confirming the hierarchal worldview of "White, then everyone else." I believe that such a practice would mirror the Trinity.

THE DENOMINATIONAL DIVIDE
(THE THIRD HURDLE)

The third hurdle is the tendency for church denominations to value their denominational clan over the collective kingdom of God. This value may have developed through theological conviction or limited experience serving with denominational outsiders. Regardless of the reasons, church networks are prone to "tests of fellowship" based on our differences instead of our one Lord, one faith, one baptism, and so on. As a result, Pentecostals may feel downright weird collaborating with Anglicans, and the church fellowship of my formative years could feel uncomfortable partnering with Presbyterians. I know plenty of Baptists who cannot stand other Baptists. The result of these differences is a conflated spirit of individualistic tribalism that hinders potential alliances.

I will never discount the great work accomplished through worldwide denominational networks. However, can we be honest? It is terrible optics to have over nine thousand church denominations while claiming to be one in Christ.[20] And how many of those denominations value collaboration with the other 8,999—or even collaborate among themselves?

In contrast, an elevated value for collaboration would prompt some interesting questions. For instance, how can local churches help each other across denominational lines to pursue their vision for the gospel? How can predominantly White congregations equitably partner with ethnic churches as a public demonstration of the gospel? Are local believers praying for one another and praying

---

20. "About Denominations," para. 2.

together for their cities, like my brother Chris Gough is doing with Light Up the City in greater Seattle?[21]

Gone should be the days when the body of Christ splinters rather than coming together in Jesus' name. Let us replace such dysfunction with "an emergent movement where believers start fighting for unity in their communities."[22]

THE RACIAL DIVIDE (THE FOURTH HURDLE)

White churches, Chinese churches, Vietnamese, Latino, and on and on—yeah, that is the fourth hurdle to consider. More than that, every denomination, to my knowledge, has church sub-alliances that are often ethnically homogeneous. They associate mainly with themselves and very seldom venture outside of their circles.

Perhaps at this moment, you feel the need to water down my observations. But, before you do, indulge me for a moment while I reminisce about some memories.

Band of Brotherhoods

Growing up in the seventies and eighties, I often heard my church fellowship describe itself as "the brotherhood." The term was confusing because my young eyes saw two brotherhoods: one White and one Black. By God's providence, my family fellowshiped and ministered in both. We attended the "White-brotherhood" events, such as Yosemite Family Encampment, an annual event attended by ten thousand believers from all over the state. We also participated in the "Black-brotherhood" events, such as the West Coast Preachers and Leaders Forum and the National Lectureship. My young, naïve, hopeful self later came to understand the more extensive disease of racism that permeated church culture. There were never two brotherhoods in our fellowship; unfortunately, we were one racially divided brotherhood. Our network was not alone

21. Light Up the City.
22. Ramirez and DeVito, *Designed for More*, 61.

in this struggle. The racial divide is a hurdle bogging down the practice of unity in the body of Christ worldwide.

THE POLITICAL DIVIDE (THE FIFTH HURDLE)

The fifth hurdle is the church's political divide. Secular politics in the church is not a new problem, but it feels more hostile than I can remember. Our vitriolic political divide destroys unity, making collaboration nearly impossible to achieve. For example, a predominantly White suburban church may view immigration differently than a largely migrant church. Their political worldviews might make church partnerships unlikely. Who could have predicted that a protective face mask would become the symbol of our current political divide? Some churches publicly condemn other churches for their mask-wearing policies. Popular Christian leaders mass distribute political statements urging congregations to resist stay-at-home orders, essentially making masks a test of fellowship. Media outlets like the *Wall Street Journal*, instead of reporting about the loving oneness of God's multiethnic church, headline their publications with politically charged statements from believers, such as "Our Lord Isn't Woke."[23] The SBC's political divide is so public that the *Wall Street Journal* reported, "No matter who wins [SBC's presidential election], the convention will have to confront the growing possibility of a schism."[24]

I have observed the bits of relational shrapnel lying around the church lobby due to Christians verbally shooting one another down in community gatherings and over social media platforms. This clash is ugly enough for long-standing members to leave their home congregations, unwelcome amid their so-called spiritual family. Politics ends friendships, gets pastors fired, and wounds families—all on full display to an onlooking world. So let me put it to you this way (modeling 1 Cor 13:1): if I have the best and only answers to make America great again but do not have love,

23. Lovett, "Our Lord Isn't Woke."
24. Lovett, "Our Lord Isn't Woke," para. 14.

I gain nothing! Furthermore, I become an obstacle to creating a collaborative culture in the body of Christ.

THE COST OF COLLABORATION
(THE SIXTH HURDLE)

The sixth hurdle is the cost of collaboration, which is often too high. Counting the price should always be considered before committing to a kingdom partnership. If members from prospective collaborative churches perceive the cost too high, the collaboration will fail. Mergers, for example, can be met with pushback like the following:

* Even if our church numbers triple, I will lose my preferred style of worship.

* Even if we become more missional, the new church will not embrace the values of my generation.

* Even if we become multiethnic, I will no longer be in the majority.

* Even if coming together is a kingdom win, too many staff members who I love may lose their jobs.

* Even if we start worshiping in the new location, I will have to drive farther than I want to on Sundays.

* Even if our church is declining, at least it is *our* church![25]

In a profit-loss analysis of local church collaboration, every church assigns value to what matters most to them. And no one wants to experience loss, even in absorption models.[26] However, unless churches become willing to give up personal and

25. These are the types of statements that I heard during my two-year case study.

26. Raymond defines "Blending by Absorption," or the absorption merger model, as follows: "Absorption occurs when a smaller church merges with a larger healthy congregation. The larger church absorbs or adopts the smaller church but doesn't change its name or its approach to ministry" (Raymond, "Churches Can Work Together," sec. 5, para. 1).

organizational agendas for the more significant objective of the *imago Dei*, this hurdle will remain a roadblock for collaboration. Most churches, in my experience, are not ready or willing to pay the price.

RECAP OF THE COLLABORATION ESSENTIALS AND HURDLES

Collaboration turned out to be more work than I had anticipated. Even with the best strategic plans, we will need the Holy Spirit's strength and guidance to shape our practice of unity so that it emulates the Holy Trinity.

Six Essentials for Collaboration Culture	Six Hurdles That Threaten Collaboration Culture
A Solid Theology	The Power Divide
A Variety of Leaders	The Privilege Divide
A High Valuing of Collaboration	The Denominational Divide
A Clear Definition and Vision	The Racial Divide
A Kingdom Mindset	The Political Divide
An Atmosphere of Prayer	The Cost of Collaboration

A WALK ON THE BEACH

So, before we take the next step in this project, I want to leave you with a pastoral word of encouragement.

Ever ask where God is?

From my apartment in Compton, take Rosecrans Avenue west until you get to Pacific Coast Highway. Turn left and keep driving until you see signs for the Redondo Beach Pier. Once you arrive, park your '77 Mustang II and head for the beach just before sunset. Walk. Listen. Just be. That is where you will find God.

So many life changes happened in 1987. The biggest was my move from the Central Valley to South Central Los Angeles (now South Los Angeles). A long-stay minister in Compton hired me part-time to lead worship and serve at large in ministry. I was excited for the opportunity and the adventure of moving away from home for the first time.

I was unprepared for the beauty of the people tempered by their daily hardships. I make no claims to being "straight out of Compton"—my experience there was ever so brief. But I proudly tell you, without reservation—

I was in way over my head and out of my element.

As if it had happened yesterday, I remember calling Dad from a pay phone after watching a daytime robbery at a check-cashing place.

I recall one particular Sunday morning when two ladies stood before the congregation during the response time. Sadly, both had been mugged on their way to worship that morning.

Members warned me never to wear red or blue shoelaces on my kicks. Police were reportedly arresting kids entering high school football games with colored shoelaces.

I also remember waking up feeling extra tired, as if I had not gotten enough sleep. Then I realized that a police helicopter was floodlighting the neighborhood. It was so bright that I thought the sun was out.

All the while, I was doing ministry. But I was lonely, depressed, and confused.

All the time.

Maybe the first time was after my other job at the UA Del Amo 6 movie theater. It might have occurred after a long Sunday. But at some point, I took off in my '77 Mustang II for the California coast. All I wanted or expected was a break from the anxiety of being far from home and the pressures of my deficiencies in ministry. Instead, what I found was unexpected and a bit difficult to explain.

I found a quiet place to meet with God.

Redondo was not noiseless. Walking on the beach, you could hear the sounds of shopkeepers and vendors selling their products. The interactive sounds of arcade games lit up and ready for action added their unmistakable vibe to the setting. All makes and models of noisy automobiles passed by on the adjacent streets. Even late at night the voices of beachcombers were still figuring out their plans to stay longer or call it a night. And the seagulls and night birds formed the background choir for everything on the pier.

But the thing that caught my attention?

That supernaturally turned all the noise into my quiet place?

The ocean waves.

That first time after sunset, I remember sitting on the beach, focused on the sound of ocean waves crashing against the wooden-pier pylons. I closed my tear-drenched eyes to heighten my senses, and I locked my hearing onto the waves dissipating into the sand. Plenty of people surrounded me with conversations and activities, but I stayed in the moment. I had no idea how desperate I had become. Nor did I thoroughly consider the severity of my circumstances. At that moment, I was not doing much thinking. Whatever I was feeling, I directed every ounce of it into one intensely focused point—the sound of real-life ocean waves.

And God met me right then and there.

Understand that I was already a certificate-carrying, baptized believer in Jesus Christ. I was an employed staff member of a local church. Yet until that one moment when I was washed over by the wafting sounds of the great Pacific, I never knew that God would meet me in my real-time situation. I had not understood his eternal invitation into his relational community. Like the Israelites wandering around the same mountain for forty years, I was saved but had not been set free.

Not only that, but God was already waiting for me once I had arrived on the beach.

He knew that I was physically exhausted and emotionally spent.

He knew that my pride would cause me to keep going until I imploded.

He knew that I loved him but was unsure that he loved me.

So he waited for me—

And I found him in the bellowing harmonies of the ocean!

My pastoral word of encouragement to all of you is this: God will never leave you or forsake you. We must keep this truth protected in our minds, spirits, and emotions. It will serve you well when our great enemy, the father of lies, whispers discouragement and doubt in your ear. And anyone who would dare pursue the heart of Christ will face challenges, lowness of spirit, and even persecution. You might face hardships and even get canceled by prominent isolationists masquerading as ecumenical partners. But know that nothing is strong enough or powerful enough to swerve you off the path of God's design for his people. He wants us to be one, and he will use you to lead the way. And all the while, he will always remain by your side. He is rooting for you, always walking with you, and forever living in you. That is the God I have come to know.

DEVOTIONAL REFLECTIONS (INDIVIDUALLY OR IN SMALL GROUPS)

1. On a scale of 1 (extremely uncomfortable) to 10 (very comfortable), describe your experience fellowshiping or working with outside churches. Write down a couple of personal examples (in small groups, share your testimonies).

2. Write down the biggest reasons why local churches seldom partner in gospel initiatives. Give a brief explanation for each hurdle (in small groups, share your response).

3. Read Rom 1:8–12, Eph 6:18, Col 1:3–14, and 2 Tim 1:3. Use your favorite translation. Allow these passages to elevate your

value of praying for the body of Christ. Spend ten to fifteen minutes highlighting your Bible or writing them down.

4. List from memory the names of local churches in your city. Commit to praying for each church at least twice in the next month. Expand your list over the same thirty days of prayer (also a small-group activity).

5. Prayer focus: "Father, stir in me a desire to pray daily for your church."

6. Song of reflection: "When We Pray" as performed by Tauren Wells.

A Prayer

Heavenly Father,

The world that you created is wonderful. We are thankful that we can be a part of it. We confess that we have not valued others as we should, especially those who are different from ourselves. We ask for your forgiveness and that we could see others as you see them. We also ask for unity in your church. Jesus, you are the head of the church, and we want to be one body. The truth, though, is that sometimes we are jealous or prideful. We want to stand under your authority and accept how you wonderfully and intentionally created each one of us. Thank you for your salvation and grace even when we fail. We love you and look forward to the day when we will all worship you together before your throne.

Amen.

Nebeský Otče,

Svět, který jsi stvořil, je nádherný. Jsme vděční za to že můžeme být toho součásti. Přiznáme se to že jsme necenili druhé jak bychom měli, obzvlášť ty, kteří jsou jiní než my. Prosíme o tvoje odpuštění a za to abychom tvými očima mohli vidět druhé jak je vidíš ty. Prosíme také o jednotu ve tvé církví. Ježíši, ty jsi hlava církve a chceme být jedno tělo. Akorát, víme že jsme někdy žárliví nebo pyšní, chceme stát pod tvou autoritou a přijímat to jak jsi nás každého nádherně a záměrně stvořil. Děkujeme za tvou spásu a milost i když selžeme. Milujeme tě a těšíme se na den jak budeme všichni tebe chválit spolu před tvým trůnem.

Amen.

Daniel Johnson
Former Missionary in Czech Republic
Middle School Pastor of Rolling Hills Community Church
Tualatin, Oregon

Chapter 7

Interviews and Reflections

Often called the 'birds-eye', ... [it] means the musician should hold the note until the conductor gives a cutoff or cue to move on to the next beat.

—FERMATA (MUSICAL SYMBOL)

SO, WHAT HAD HAPPENED WAS . . .

SEAN CONNERY'S ICONIC MALONE in Brian DePalma's *The Untouchables* walked Special Agent Eliot Ness to the post office to execute a Chicago-style liquor raid. Even more audacious was that the backroom hooch factory was across the street from the police station. Ness was stunned by their inability to take down Capone's well-known operation. Malone's explanation was classic: "Mr. Ness, everybody knows where the booze is. The problem isn't finding it; the problem is who wants to cross Capone."[1] Ness, as it turned out, was the right man for the job.

---

1. Untouchables (1987), sec. 15.

When I chose my final thesis topic, two guiding observations played pivotal roles. I have mentioned both throughout this project.

> First, the twenty-first-century church is not one. We profess oneness while our lived experiences misalign with our biblical theology—and this grieves our Lord.
>
> Second, Christian pastors and leaders do not value church collaboration enough, which crimps their interest in pursuing partnerships.

Similar to the "Chicago way," these two observations are common knowledge among my mentors and colleagues. The problem is not knowing these observations; the problem is who wants to disrupt systemic disunity and build a worldwide culture of collaboration.

I do.

How about you?

LET ME CALL A FRIEND

During my project, I reached out to thirty-four Christian influencers across the nation and requested interviews on local church collaboration. Thirty-two of them granted my request. In this final chapter, we will engage with those interviews.

Participants included professional church pastors, Christian lay leaders, and professional Christian educators. Our interviews occurred in person, over the phone, and in online chats between July 10 and September 4, 2019.[2]

Four main issues framed our discussions and shaped my final reflections about collaboration. They included:

* the value placed on collaboration by local churches and their leaders

* the barriers to collaboration

* the solutions to overcome collaboration barriers

2. See appendix A, table A-1 for the complete list.

* the metrics for successful partnerships

Admittedly, thirty-two interviews were not a large-enough sample size to accurately assess the state of evangelical churches on these four issues. However, the interviewee pool was pretty diverse. Participants represented eight denominations or networks.[3] Roles included fourteen lead/senior church pastors, eight staff pastors, eight lay leaders, five church planters, two seminary deans, six parachurch leaders, and one missionary. Collectively, they represented ten ethnicities,[4] eight states, and two countries.

Our conversations highlighted the four rhythms of collaboration (relationships, trust, diversity, and inclusion) related to building healthy, sustainable kingdom partnerships. With my two guiding observations in mind, I hoped the interviewees would identify noticeable factors that reduce or elevate the level of value one places on collaboration. They did so admirably.

Also, the participants' input was invaluable in helping shape this model's four rhythms. Two pastors in particular offered wise counsel to differentiate between diversity and inclusion, which was missing in early drafts of the model.[5]

Also, it was beneficial to learn that other Christian leaders have seen similar trends, experienced similar challenges, and reached similar conclusions about the essentials and hurdles of collaboration.

Another consideration was the plausibility that this model was too idealistic for most churches to implement. Discussing this concern with frontline church leaders confirmed that the model was on the right track yet could improve. Their input helped gauge

3. Interviewees represent the following denominations or networks: Christian Church (Disciples of Christ), Nondenominational, Nondenominational/Indian Christian Fellowship, Southern Baptist Convention, Calvary Chapel, Nondenominational/Colossae Church Network, Churches of Christ, and Evangelical Presbyterian Church.

4. Interviewees represent the following ethnicities: White, South Asian/Indian, Vietnamese, Cuban, Chinese, Korean, Jewish, Japanese, Filipino, and Iranian.

5. Interviews with Paul Kroger from Mosaic Church in Little Rock, Arkansas, and Adam Paa from The Village Church in Flower Mound, Texas.

how this model could assist local congregations in developing a ubiquitous culture of trinitarian collaboration.

With that, here are a few highlights and ten reflections that came from our conversations.

LET'S TALK VALUES

One question on the interview questionnaire asked participants about values.

"What are the top values for your ministry context?"[6]

Five of the thirty-two interviewees responded with "unity in Christ" or "partnerships." None of the rest said that collaboration was one of their top values. Every interviewee said that "big-C Church" unity is part of their overall gospel identity, meaning solidarity in Christ. However, they also said that collaboration was not a normative practice; and that it did not resonate with the vision of their ministry context. As one interviewee said, "If it happens, it happens." Their comments led me to the following two reflections.

FIRST REFLECTION

Members of Common Ground experienced their most energized seasons of ministry while partnering with other churches. Perhaps their values of community, relationships, and diversity are contributing reasons. Most attendees would say that the potential for collaboration was the main reason God moved CG to central Beaverton. Three months after relocating to the campus, we participated in a combined Christmas Eve morning service with all six congregations. Listening to "Silent Night" sung in all of those languages was spectacular! Other collaborations included an area-wide worship night, an annual "trunk or treat" (alternative Halloween event), collecting socks for the homeless in downtown Portland, an "adopt-a-roadway" event on our neighborhood street, and a longer list of other events and activities. Each combined

6. See appendix A, table A-2.

event complemented CG's vision and created an atmosphere of anticipation.

On reflection, our multi-church endeavors reminded Common Ground of our kingdom connection in this valley. The other congregations needed the same reminder. Every believer should occasionally experience collaborative events packed with enthusiastic Christians wanting to honor God to the fullest. To some degree, we are all rehearsing the glorious celebration that will one day commence in glory around the throne of God.

SECOND REFLECTION

On the other hand, we did not fully grasp how pursuing collaboration could be a gospel strategy in our twenty-first-century world. We acknowledge the Great Commission as our gospel mission but struggle with accomplishing it effectively—just like other communities of faith. Considering CG's strengths of hospitality, diversity, and relationships, pursuing collaboration is something we *can* do and *love* to do. Members even felt disappointment when our collaborative opportunities became steadily more infrequent.

On reflection, I am hopeful that CG will resee our culture of collaboration as part of our gospel mission.

If the Great Commandment says, "I love you"—

If the Great Commission says, "Let me tell you how much God loves you"[7]—

perhaps the great calling of the twenty-first-century church will be a collaboration that says, "Let us show you how God loves you by the way we love one another."

7. This is a paraphrase of Richard, "Great Commission," para. 7–8.

LET'S TALK BARRIERS TO COLLABORATION

Another question on the interview questionnaire focused on hurdles: "In your opinion, what are the barriers that prevent local churches from collaborating with one another?"[8]

What was striking about this question was that the answers varied and were broadly spread. So, a key to gaining insight from this variance was to look for the common thread.

Every interviewee,[9] either directly or indirectly, focused on the importance of building relationships. For example, Reg Cox, former senior minister and current director of Lakewood Connects, said, "Change or progress moves at the speed of relationships." He has also learned that "people will come to faith in Christ through relationships and friendships." Dr. Bruce Fong, dean of Dallas Theological Seminary in Houston, Texas, said barriers to collaboration include "competition factors, insecurity of pastors, and racial issues." Dan Jocoy, minister and equipper of Tri-Cities Church of Christ in Myrtle Creek, Oregon, replied that some leaders have too much "pride to be teachable." Instead, as a leader, you ought to "believe that others have something to speak into your life or ministry." Dan McClure, the former lead pastor of First Christian Church in Palo Alto, California, answered that "pride, competition, theology, and denominationalism" are barriers preventing local church collaboration. Mike Harrison, senior pastor of Parkland Chapel in Farmington, Missouri, said, "Fear, the inconvenience of collaborating (relationships, lack of time, etc.), and [the fact that] smaller churches do not have enough members to risk losing them through collaborative events." From Beaverton, Oregon, Matt Bowen, lead pastor of Emmaus Church, responded, "The personalities of the leaders involved." Daniel Johnson, former college-student missionary for Josiah Adventures in the Czech Republic, responded with an analogy. He compared local church

---

8. See appendix A, table A-3.

9. The titles and locations for interviewees reflect current roles and positions. Some have changed since our interview period between July 10 and September 4, 2019.

leaders in Olomouc to competing opticians. One leader specializes in eyeglass sales while a second leader specializes in contact-lens sales. Both have the same clientele—people who need their vision corrected. However, pride prevents them from working together, even while being self-aware of their deficiencies. Ikki Soma, lead pastor of Bayou City Fellowship in Houston, Texas, talked about "territorialism." In one instance, area church leaders disputed over who was in charge of a community garden. Another dispute at a different church escalated into a fistfight during a funeral. All of these responses point to a missing relational component that prevented churches from working together. They prompted the following three reflections.

THIRD REFLECTION

Churches with shared values collaborate best. Initially, I assumed that partnering with six congregations on the same campus was an automatic home run. That assumption was wrong! I grossly underestimated the angst that church families feel to protect and preserve their narratives, identity, culture, vision, and practices— and the threat that collaboration poses to all of them. I did not fully understand the importance of first entering a dialogue about collaboration with leaders who already valued it.

On reflection, our campus pastors had varying values for collaboration. We shared a theology of union with Christ but needed more practice initiating relationships. Perhaps the Holy Spirit can use me to intentionally invite them into a consistent pattern of togetherness in Christ. Such unity, in my opinion, remains an underutilized strategy for gospelizing our world.

FOURTH REFLECTION

The congregations most willing to collaborate were those whose pastors had good relationships. This formula laid the groundwork for creating a kingdom-minded, collaborative culture. Why? Their respective members felt that if their pastors were friends, maybe they could venture an occasional ministry partnership or worship together. They even expressed confusion about why their respective communities were not collaborating more often.

On reflection, why would anyone expect their churches to fellowship together if their influential leaders are not modeling relationships? Interviewees unanimously emphasized the importance of relationships in kingdom work, especially among pastors. Their comments affirmed the need for effective partnerships to build on a relational foundation.

FIFTH REFLECTION

Even though seven congregations met weekly on the same campus, only a few people built cross-congregational relationships during my case study. The campus pastors, in my opinion, could have done a better job leading in this area. Speaking only for CG, two years seemed like plenty of time to learn names, recognize faces, schedule coffee meetings, book playdates for kids, and so on. Members would occasionally ask me how other pastors were doing, even though they could easily ask them directly. After all, they would likely see them in the church lobby on the following Sunday!

On reflection, I wonder to what degree I modeled cross-congregational relationships but fell short in equipping others to do the same. This project will serve as an equipping resource moving forward. In addition, our church relationships were cordial but confined to activities on campus. How deep can friendships grow if restricted to infrequent, three-minute conversations between worship services? More quality time together would have provided opportunities to share spiritual testimonies, ministry insights, creative ideas for city outreach, family burdens, and more. These types of interactions could have led to more relational trust. I maintain that believers familiar with one another serve better in collaborative ministry. Those efforts produce more joy and fulfillment. Increasing the relational aspect of the joint endeavors would glorify God as much as (if not more than) any single ministry ever could.

LET'S TALK SOLUTIONS TO OVERCOME COLLABORATION BARRIERS

A question on the questionnaire asked interviewees the following: "What are your solutions for local churches to overcome collaboration barriers?"[10]

Ed Glinden, former recovery-ministry pastor of Central Peninsula Church in Foster City, California, suggested "pastor pulpit exchanges, pastors building relationships, and pastors serving together" in hands-on ministries in their cities. Tom Greene, lay teacher and small-group leader of Shoreline Church in Monterey, California, said collaboration must become part of the local church's mission. Understanding the path toward partnerships can help churches pursue opportunities to engage their trust, meaning collaboration. Keivan Tehrani, Global Compassion pastor of Westgate Church in San Jose, California, suggested "creating more pastor networks along affinity lines like race, denomination, theology, etc." He argued for a stronger gospel connection among city pastors: "What about the desperation for the overwhelming masses going to hell—is not motivation enough?" Dr. Derek Chinn, dean of Multnomah Biblical Seminary in Portland, Oregon, said, "Leaders can model collaboration through relinquishing power." Samuel Middlebrook, the former pastor of Graceroots Community Church in Yakima, Washington, suggested that pastors should "find out what other churches are doing and ask what they can do to help." Sudha Peethala, lead pastor of India International Church in Hillsboro, Oregon, said, "Pastors should do more biblical teaching that we are neither Jew nor Greek, slave or free, male or female, but that we are one in Christ." These responses capture the overall sentiment of every interviewee regarding the question of barrier solutions. Here are my resulting two reflections.

10. See appendix A, table A-4.

SIXTH REFLECTION

Our collective churches were inconsistent in committing our potential collaborations to prayer. We needed "effective" prayer by expectant believers convinced that God's power would show up in mighty ways (Jas 5:16). The word "effective" is an English translation from the Greek word ενεργούμενη (*energoúmeni*), a form of ἐνεργέω (*energéō*). It means "to be operative, be at work, put forth power; to work for one, aid one; to effect; to display one's activity, show one's self operative."[11] Imagine if we had collectively prayed, "Father, may the gospel be displayed throughout our city as a result of our togetherness in Christ." Such a prayerful submission may have convinced leaders that collaboration was the work God wanted us to do.

On reflection, I wonder how things would have changed if would-be collaborators had sought God's face through effectual, fervent prayer. What would have happened if every congregation prayed daily for one another and weekly with one another? What if the entire campus were a house of effectual, fervent prayer? There is also the relational component to praying for the body. Jesus knew this when he taught, "First be reconciled to your brother, and then come and offer your gift" (Matt 5:23–24). The act of mending relationships brings us closer to the objective of being one. Our campus churches missed out on valuable opportunities to strengthen relationships by worshiping God through prayer. But we can certainly change, and so can the other Christian churches in our cities. A renewed commitment to praying with and for one another is something that every local church can do. This observation leads to a very challenging reflection that will require forgiveness and repentance in addition to prayer.

---

11. *Strong's Lexicon*, s.v. "*energéō*," https://www.blueletterbible.org/lexicon/g1754/esv/mgnt/0-1/.

SEVENTH REFLECTION

Leaders must resolve conflict before considering collaboration. Misunderstandings and miscommunications happen all the time but can quickly get out of control if left unresolved. Those types of wounds, without relational trust, exacerbate then sour the likelihood of future partnerships. Our campus ran into collaboration hurdles like pride, fear, lack of relationships, and mistrust. Yet all was not lost—not even close! What we needed was a season of forgiveness, repentance, and prayer prompted and led by the Holy Spirit. After all, the church gains nothing if we build large collaborative ministries but fail to love one another.[12] Thank God that we are all works in progress. I am hopeful we will get there in Jesus' name.

LET'S TALK METRICS FOR SUCCESSFUL COLLABORATION

The last question asked from the questionnaire was "When local churches collaborate, how should they measure success?"[13]

Just like the previous questions, respondents' top measurements for success were relationship based. Rob Schulze, executive pastor of Peninsula Bible Church in Palo Alto, said that "trust, yearly evaluations, long-term vision, and a healthy balance between mission and relationships" are better metrics for success in local church collaboration. In Sunnyvale, California, Dr. Joel King, lead pastor of Trinity Church, believes that the trust built through collaboration benefits spiritual discipleship: "Collaborative discussions can lead to affirmation and rethinking of one's own theological beliefs and practices." David Odell, pastor of First Baptist Church in The Dalles, Oregon, said that we should measure collaboration by the way local pastors relinquish power. Odell said it like this: "I must decrease so that others can increase."[14]

12. See the apostle Paul's comments on love in 1 Cor 13:1–3.

13. See appendix A, table A-5.

14. Odell is referring to the quotation from John the Baptist in John 3:30,

Several interviewees agreed that actualized collaboration was the best metric for collaboration. It was interesting to note that fifteen interviewees did not (or could not) offer an experience or opinion on the metrics for collaboration. However, all of them believe that relationships are essential in building kingdom partnerships. My conclusion from these responses is that pursuing relationships is part of their success metrics, though they did not state it directly. Their comments led to my final three reflections.

EIGHTH REFLECTION

The interviewees identified "actualized collaboration" as one metric for successful collaboration. Our seven campus churches did work together in ministry from time to time. We had varying degrees of buy-in and challenges, but collaboration did occur. I should never overlook this or miss an opportunity to give God praise. Now what? Since this collaboration model mirrors the loving community of the Trinity, we must never stop short of the mark (unity) to claim victory (we did stuff together).

On reflection, collaborating church leaders should take on the responsibility of keeping the public display of the gospel as the primary metric for successful collaboration. When people see our love for one another (unity), they believe that the Father sent Jesus. Anything less than this is a reduction of the type of collaboration promoted in this project.

NINTH REFLECTION

God's word says, "Behold, how good and pleasant it is when brothers dwell in unity" (Ps 133:1). I fondly remember how Dad embodied visionary leadership that consistently promoted goodwill among believers. No matter the occasion or type of church brand,

---

where John is elevating Christ above himself before the crowds. Similarly, Odell believes that when local pastors follow this example, they relinquish their personal ideals, preferences, agendas, etc. as a practical demonstration of the gospel through kingdom partnerships in their communities.

he went out of his way to share Christ's heart for his people—to love one another and persevere through inevitable conflicts and hardships.

On reflection, God was pleased every time our campus congregations fellowshiped together in unity. Our togetherness was an offering of worship to God. We should celebrate this and thank God for the work he placed on our hearts. In addition, I pray that we will recognize how primed the "big-C Church" is for a brand-new movement of the Spirit of God. This movement will be a revival marked by new kingdom relationships, newly developed trust, intentional diversity, and unique invitations for inclusive voices to join the gospel mission. I want to be part of such a revival, for it is the kind that promotes the heart of Christ!

TENTH REFLECTION

I wonder what would have happened if our campus churches had embraced this model for collaboration.

What if every pastor agreed to initiate relationships, define expectations, discuss potential barriers, confess fears, admit pride, study God's word with others, commit to prayer, and so on?

What if we modeled our collaboration after the perfect communion of the Father, Son, and Holy Spirit?

What if our respective congregations followed our lead?

On reflecting specifically about our context, I pray that the Lord spiritually renews our connected hearts to cultivate new soil in central Beaverton. He has the power to accomplish this—no doubt in my mind. Being like him has always been the objective, not working a new model to grow our churches. Our God is perfect, even though our ministry models have their quirks and flaws. We will encounter challenges and conflicts, but this model may keep us on the path toward practicing unity.

TWELVE RECOMMENDATIONS

For those readers looking to begin collaboration, this project is good news. It offers the following twelve recommendations for church leaders to consider before entering into collaboration as a practice of unity. This list was composed of observations from my case study and is in no particular order.

1. Every church will not be able to collaborate with everyone, but every church ought to collaborate with someone! Recognize how your public display of unity influences your neighbor's receptivity to the gospel. Change the tide from optional collaboration to standard practice in the twenty-first-century church.

2. Gospel collaborations are more effective when their visionary leaders have preestablished relational trust. Congregations that skip or dismiss this foundational rhythm tend to have shorter-lived partnerships.

3. Most pastors and church leaders have low values for collaboration. So, a starting point for your church to collaborate may be to build up this value in your leaders. When possible, encourage them to acquire fresh biblical insights and collaborative experiences that increase their appraisal of multi-church endeavors.

4. Potential collaborators need a clear definition of collaboration. Therefore, leaders must dedicate time to align their respective descriptions and visions for collaboration.

5. Incorporating collaboration into pastors' job descriptions provides emotional freedom for pastors to practice unity without the fear of losing their jobs. So, consider how your church can define space for your leaders to pursue collaborative relationships in measurable and meaningful ways.

6. Churches need biblical directives for collaboration. Consider planning a "lecture-lab" sermon series that features the four rhythms of collaboration. Also, consider leading practical

experiences that help your leaders and members collaborate with other local congregations.

7. Leaders should intentionally teach their people that collaboration is much more than cohabitation. Communities of faith meeting on the same campus or in the same city can still be segregated and siloed.

8. Church collaboration without an atmosphere of prayer is problematic and highly ineffective. So, regularly engage leaders in prayer and solicit their spiritual discernment about potential partnerships in your city.

9. Potential collaborators must address their inherent power dynamics or risk sabotaging their future partnerships. My strong advice is to have those tough, awkward conversations *now* to open doors for collaboration to follow.

10. Leaders of racial reconciliation could benefit from an intentional practice of initiating relationships, building trust, celebrating diversity, and inviting inclusion. But regardless of who you are, take on the mantle of racial reconciliation. Pursue with intent both diverse engagement and inclusion of that diversity in your leadership. If you do, you and your team will mirror the Trinity!

11. Most ethnically homogenous congregations are more diverse than they realize. Your differences can include educational backgrounds, socioeconomic factors, spiritual giftings, experiences, and much more. God brought a beautiful variety of people to your congregation for his purposes. Identify and celebrate your congregation's diversity. Invite their input into your gospel agenda.

12. Collaboration is not easy, so prepare for the long haul. Then get ready to celebrate every step along the way. Examples of things to celebrate include (a) understanding your challenges, (b) counting the cost, (c) overcoming relational hurts and injuries, (d) discovering easier collaborations, (e) learning

how to collaborate better, and eventually (f) modeling collaboration for your city and the kingdom!

CONCLUSION

Christian pastors, leaders, and educators have an unprecedented opportunity to rethink how to be the "big-C Church" in a post-Christian world if we choose to accept the assignment. The gospel should never take a back seat to the pursuits of local congregations implementing church-growth strategies. Twenty-one years into the twenty-first century, we need local church leaders to be part of a spiritually awakened generation that recognizes they can no longer be the church on their own. Butler is right: "Doing it alone won't work anymore."[15]

Moving the body of Christ toward this path requires a recalibration of how we measure "church success."

The prevalent metric in evangelical churches is to be well-run, siloed American business corporations with CEOs, a board of directors, shareholders, executives, articles of incorporation, business plans, bylaws, and so on.[16]

This project's metric is for churches to ever increase their practice of oneness in their cities until collaboration becomes the air we breathe.

Therein lie the players in a tale of two mirrors.

The world is full of churches longing for the reality of the first mirror's reflection. Some achieve it, while others stare longingly into that mirror, hoping to become a thriving church one day. Over my ministry career, I have watched churches focus the lion's share of their time and energy on growing their respective congregations (staffing, Sunday programming, finances, Christian education, calendaring, business meetings, etc.). Less obvious was

15. Butler, *Well Connected*, 299.

16. See Reed, "Corporate Governance" for a description of how American corporations are run. I have drawn from Reed's description, applying it to the way churches are often run in the US.

determining how their siloed efforts impacted their cities for the gospel. No doubt every congregation touches lives in Jesus' name. Yet, most of us take our best gospel resource too lightly—the other churches in our cities.

So, here is the challenge of this project to Christian leaders everywhere:

* Initiate new kingdom relationships, build new trust narratives, celebrate diversity, and intentionally include diverse voices in your gospel mission.

* Commit to the hard work of becoming one while our nation navigates a racial reckoning.

* Reimagine trinitarian collaboration as the new measure of church success.

* Leverage the practice of unity so that your biblical theology matches our daily reality.

Then our twenty-first-century citizens will have heightened recognition of Jesus Christ as Lord of all.

Oh yeah—

And drink a lot more coffee!

DEVOTIONAL REFLECTIONS
(INDIVIDUALLY OR IN SMALL GROUPS)

1. Read 1 Cor 13 in its entirety. Ask the Lord to use it to frame your thoughts about the unity of believers. Which verses (or words) capture your attention? Spend ten to fifteen minutes highlighting them in your Bible or writing them down.

2. What are your spiritual gifts or the hobbies/activities that give you joy? Pray and ask God to show you how/where to use your gift(s) to initiate relationships, build trust, celebrate diversity, and invite inclusion. Then, journal your reflections (in small groups, share them).

3. Reread the section "Twelve Recommendations" in this chapter. Are any of these actionable recommendations that resonate with your church? If so, identify them and write down some ways to put them into action (in small groups, share/compare suggestions).

4. Visit a local church's website and locate their contact page. Please spend a few minutes sending them a short, encouraging message. Let them know that a fellow believer is rooting for them in Jesus' name. Write the church's name plus the date and time you contacted them. Ask God to keep them in your prayerful heart.

5. Plan to visit a local worship service. The chances are good that you will find a service that does not conflict with your home-church gathering. Ask the Lord to increase your heart connection to the body of Christ as a result of your visit. Write down reflections from your visit (in small groups, share your experience).

6. List from memory the names of local pastors/church leaders in your city. Then, commit to praying for each of them at least twice in the next month. Then, expand your list over the same thirty days of prayer (also a small-group activity).

7. Prayer focus: "God in heaven, show me the collaborative work that you have placed on my path."

8. Song of reflection: "Build Your Kingdom Here" as performed by Rend Collective.

THREE PRAYERS

Lord,

We cry out to you, our heavenly Father, who knows us, loves us, and longs for us to be united as your people. May we see with your eyes, Lord, and wear your name as our banner. Rather than being quick to judge, may we be quick to love. Rather than seeing our differences, may we see our similarities. Holy Spirit, stir in us the desire to live peacefully with others, to show compassion, gentleness, and humility towards others. Go before us and behind us. Live within us and around us. We come before you knowing you hear our prayers, and we live with great expectation of a day when your people are united as the family of God. Amen.

> Kerry and Lori VanDer Kamp
> Common Ground Church
> Beaverton, Oregon

God, our heavenly Father,

Thank you for your love to mankind: wishing that none of us should perish but that we all, through your beloved Son (Jesus), inherit everlasting life.

We know that one of the strategies Satan is using to hinder the spread of your gospel is sowing seeds of division amongst your children. By the authority given to us by Jesus Christ, we stand against the spirit of division, bigotry, and hatred amongst believers. We resist pride amongst the body of Christ. We pray that as servants of God, we shall see each other as children of the same Father God and treat each other with love, irrespective of denominational differences. I pray that we shall support and pray for each other so that the world will know that we are indeed serving the same living God, will believe in our message, and will seek to know God.

Gracious God, forgive us for falling short in many areas: for criticizing our fellow brethren instead of praying for them. Help us to be more compassionate to one another, humbler, and more willing to learn. Help us to seek guidance whenever we are confused.

Above all, may the Holy Spirit continue to dwell in us. Give us the strength and courage to continue working in your vineyard. May your kingdom come.

In Jesus' name, amen.

Emmanuel N. Epie
Common Ground Church
Beaverton, Oregon (originally from Nyasoso, Southwest Region, Cameroon, Central Africa)

Heavenly Father,

May your name be praised among all people and all nations! Though we speak in different tongues and have differing cultures and subcultures, the blood of your Son and the power of the Holy Spirit bind us together as *one*, just as you are three in one. Please forgive us when we have been motivated by selfish ambition or worldly agendas. We, as the church, desire to be your witnesses to unity as one body and one spirit bonded by humility, gentleness, and peace. In the name of Jesus, we pray against the enemy that seeks to destroy and divide and tear down what we build up. We rely on you, Father, to lead and direct us as the head that moves this body with all of our different gifts and functions. We can only work well together because of you, Lord!

Amen.

Jen Man
Common Ground Church (repping loud and proud!)
Beaverton, Oregon

Epilogue

Silence

This is the symbol for silence. It marks the passage of time for the
musician while they don't play.

—Rest (musical symbol)

This entire book was an invitation to do something different.

Change the course of our pursuit to be one.

Now, let me tell you how to bring all of it to a screeching halt.

There is a stealthy weapon powerful enough to sabotage the
work of Christian unity and wound believers in its blast radius.

Silence.

Throughout the writing of this material, I witnessed an unprecedented racial reckoning in America and around the world.
And I must acknowledge the impact that this singular moment
in time played on this love assignment. I claim no expertise on
matters of race and justice (except living for fifty-six years), nor
was this project designed to speak primarily to these issues. Yet,
presenting a finished product without any allusion to the racial
elephant in the room would be wrong. So, please stick with me
during this post-Juneteenth epilogue. Perhaps we can learn from
our past troubles while taking steps toward oneness in Christ.

LOUD SILENCE

Ask a Black believer, "What hurt you the most in 2020?" and prepare to hear many of them say, "The silence."

Why did silence wound us so deeply?

Because it came from people we thought were family!

Usually, silence is void of sound. But this particular silence had volume and depth that left a lasting impression. It was like expecting a massive dubstep drop but having your AirPods' batteries die right before the drop. An older analogy would be like waiting for cymbal crashes that never came during the William Tell Overture. But instead, it was a "here it comes, where did it go?" moment that sucked the life out of the strongest of men and the toughest of women. It was palpable silence—a missed opportunity that left Black believers wondering, "My brother, my sister, why did you forsake me?" And when the dust settled, all forward motion of unity or reconciliation shattered to bits while silence stood in the corner with folded arms, wondering, "What was I supposed to do? Were you expecting me to say something?"

IT AIN'T THAT COMPLICATED

We wanted the truth of Scripture to match our realities: "There is neither Jew nor Greek, there is neither slave nor free, there is no male and female, for you are all one in Christ Jesus" (Gal 3:28).

However, they do not match.

And the latest evidence from the racial reckoning?

Black brothers and sisters cried out (and I mean *cried out*) for justice. We grieved over the public showcasing of lives cut short. Moms and dads groaned with the kind of anguish no parent should ever have to bear. Yet, while Black brothers and sisters wailed and pleaded for change, our White and multicultural evangelical church at large were inexplicably silent.

And in the world?

Those lost sinners, who need our Christian message so severely, took to the streets by the thousands. They demanded that America finally treat Black lives as rightful heirs to its creeds:

> We hold these truths to be self-evident, that all men are created equal, that their Creator endows them with certain unalienable Rights, that among these are Life, Liberty and the pursuit of Happiness.[1]

The world spoke up. Black believers wanted their White brothers and sisters to do the same. Some did so, but most remained loudly silent.

And that is not how families should treat one another.

MOM'S WISDOM

I was venting to my seventy-four-year-old mom, Adella, about this subject. She patiently listened to me emote over the slow or nonexistent response of non-Black Christian leaders across the nation. Of course, that led to a verbal litany of disappointments and unmet expectations, some of which I did not realize were personal wounds. I shook out of it and suddenly realized that I was dumping my garbage on Mom; I quickly apologized for being an idiot. After a pause, Mom stopped me in my tracks with her words. I always appreciate her attentive listening skills and wise advice. Here is my paraphrase of her timely wisdom:

> Don't worry about it, Baby. That is what families are for—to be there for one another. That's what families do. They want to be there through the joys and the pains. You don't owe me an apology, son. That's what it means to be family.

Wow!

I froze for several seconds. Mom put into words what many Black Christians have been feeling for decades. Family should always be there for each other. Bryan Loritts stated a similar

---

1. Jefferson et al., "Declaration of Independence," para. 2.

sentiment: "Family and friendship are not synonymous. Your family is who you are responsible for. You don't choose family. You choose friends. Churches are families, where people must feel responsible for each other. In your church, friendships may happen, but family must happen."[2] Therein lies the core component of our hurt from 2020. We thought that *everyone* in God's church was family. But the silence in response to injustices committed against us left some of us in doubt.

BIBLICAL EXAMPLES OF LOUD SILENCE

Loud silence is not new. Do you recall Cain avoiding God's question about the location of his brother? "Then the Lord said to Cain, 'Where is Abel your brother?' He said, 'I do not know; am I my brother's keeper'" (Gen 4:9b)?

I bet Abel, murdered by his brother (Gen 4:8), heard Cain's silence.

Abraham told Pharaoh and Abimelech that Sarah was his sister. He spoke to save himself but not to protect his faithful wife (Gen 12:13; 20:2).

I bet Sarah, sacrificed as a human shield, felt her husband's silence.

Young Joseph gave a favorable dream interpretation to his jail mate, the king's chief cupbearer. But rather than repay him upon his reinstatement, "the chief cupbearer did not remember Joseph, but forgot him" (Gen 40:23).

I bet Joseph, languishing in jail for a crime he did not commit, grieved the cupbearer's silence.

The impatient, rebellious Israelites told Moses' brother Aaron to "make us gods who shall go before us" (Exod 32:1b). However, instead of demanding that they obey the Lord that brought them out of the land of Egypt, he made excuses to Moses to deflect his participation in the rebellion: "And Aaron said [to Moses], 'Let not the anger of my lord burn hot. You know the people, that they are

---

2. Loritts, "Family and friendship."

set on evil'" (Exod 32:22). Nevertheless, God subsequently sent a plague on the people "because they made the calf" (Exod 32:35).

I bet the Israelites recognized how Aaron's silence contributed to their suffering.

God instructed Jonah, "'Arise, go to Nineveh, that great city, and call out against it, for their evil has come up before me'" (Jonah 1:2). Instead of Jonah using his voice to warn the people of the impending wrath, "[he] rose to flee to Tarshish from the presence of the Lord" (Jonah 1:3).

I bet Jonah, withering away in the belly of a great fish (Jonah 1:17), regretted his silence.

Bartimaeus cried out for messianic mercy: "Jesus, Son of David, have mercy on me!" But instead of supporting this blind beggar, Mark's Gospel says, "many rebuked him, telling him to be silent" (Mark 10:47b, 48a).

I bet Bartimaeus remembered the day his fellow countrymen pressured him to keep silent.

While Caiaphas, the high priest, interrogated Jesus, Peter hid in the crowd waiting in the courtyard. He had three opportunities to speak on behalf of Jesus. Instead, while the Son of God was spat on, mocked, and beaten by his people, Peter refused to speak for Jesus and denied knowing him (Matt 26:57–75).

I bet a rooster's crow forever reminded Peter that his silence had left Jesus all alone.

Pontius Pilate, a seasoned politician, knew that Jesus was not guilty of the charges against him. He had the vested power of Caesar to release anyone of his choosing. But instead, "when Pilate saw that he was gaining nothing, but rather that a riot was beginning, he took water and washed his hands before the crowd, saying, 'I am innocent of this man's blood; see to it yourselves.' And all the people answered, 'His blood be on us and on our children!' Then he released for them Barabbas, and having scourged Jesus, delivered him to be crucified" (Matt 27:26–26).

I bet the governor's silence hounded his mind and emotions with a guilty conscience.

In these few examples, the silence was not a nonaction; it was a self-preserving action that protected individual interests while leaving others exposed to danger or pain. Whether intentional or unintentional, these biblical characters damaged lives. Sure, God can heal pain, restore loss, and even raise the innocent from the dead. Nevertheless, their perpetrated damage made tectonic impacts on relationships.

SIGNS OF THE IMPACT OF SILENCE

What about the impact of silence in today's world? When I saw the new statistic from Barna's Beyond Diversity report—"Almost three in 10 Black practicing Christians in a multiracial church (29%) say they have experienced racial prejudice on some level"[3]—my honest reaction was "That percentage seems low." And then I read, "More than one-quarter of Black practicing Christians feels pressured to give up part of their racial or ethnic identity in a multiracial church (27%) and finds it difficult to build relationships here (28%),"[4] and my next thought was "Is that all? I would have guessed a lot more."

Why?

Leaving Because of the Pressure

Some believers feel pressure to mute their coloration in White and multiethnic churches. Being lesser versions of our God-created selves is exhausting work while having no real payoff. In the end, silence breaks hearts.

I know the nauseating hints from church leaders who wanted me to soften (or darken) my Blackness to keep my ministry job. As a people pleaser in recovery, it is even more draining to be *too Black* for some churches and *not Black enough* for others. Barna's report seems to indicate that other Black believers experience

3. "Multiracial Churches," para. 3.
4. "Multiracial Churches," para. 5.

similar pressure. As a result, many are now searching for new spiritual communities to connect with other believers that will fully accept them.

A Personal Example of the Pressure

In the early 1990s, I received an invitation to lead worship for a Christian university's national lectureship. At the planning meeting, the director complimented my worship-leading style but offered me some strong advice. He said I should adjust my style to lead more effectively at this prestigious event. I will never forget his exact words: "Avery, you need to be more 'dignified.'" His subsequent explanation of "dignified" told me that I needed to be *less loud, less soulful,* and *a lot less undignified than usual.* I understood—he was not the first church leader to school me about being Black in White settings. So, the event arrived, and—if I recall correctly—I respectfully ignored him and got my praise on!

But can you understand my pressure?

To be accepted as an equal member of God's family?

There is a massive difference between "We are fully family because of Christ" and "Come hang out with us for a few years. We will evaluate how well you adjust to our way of doing things. Eventually, we will let you know if you are a right fit for our family." The former is the unmet dream; the latter is the reality. We still have some distance to travel to be the church through the eyes of Jesus.

Even in this complicated reality, God must have a way forward. Let me share with you what I am learning as a student of the eternal King.

BOOKS, YES! AND?

The church needs a new path forward to help us lament the hurtful silence. We must live into our designed purpose as the body of Christ—to be one. Reading more books on race and having more discussions about reconciliation can be constructive first steps.

Then what? Otherwise, book suggestions can feel like "doing the same thing over and over again and expecting different results."[5] Sadly, Christians loving one another as the family of God is not the norm. If Christians recommitted themselves to doing this, things would be different.

A REALIZED FAMILY OF BELIEVERS

Here are several texts that describe how the family of believers *should* respond to one another:

> For just as the body is one and has many members, and all the members of the body, though many, are one body, so it is with Christ. . . . If one member suffers, all suffer together; if one member is honored, all rejoice together. Now you are the body of Christ and individually members of it. (1 Cor 12:12, 26–27)

> This is my commandment, that you love one another as I have loved you. Greater love has no one than this, that someone lay down his life for his friends. (John 15:12–13)

> Rejoice with those who rejoice, weep with those who weep. Live in harmony with one another. Do not be haughty, but associate with the lowly. Never be wise in your own sight. (Rom 12:15–16)

> We who are strong have an obligation to bear with the failings of the weak, and not to please ourselves. (Rom 15:1)

> Blessed be the God and Father of our Lord Jesus Christ, the Father of mercies and God of all comfort, who comforts us in all our affliction, so that we may be able to comfort those who are in any affliction, with the comfort with which we ourselves are comforted by God. (2 Cor 1:3–4)

5. This phrase is often attributed to Albert Einstein, although there is no conclusive evidence that he actually said it (Pruitt, "Albert Einstein," para. 5).

Do nothing from rivalry or conceit, but in humility count others more significant than yourselves. (Phil 2:3)

Yet it was kind of you to share my trouble. (Phil 4:14)

Put on then, as God's chosen ones, holy and beloved, compassionate hearts, kindness, humility, meekness, and patience, bearing with one another and, if one has a complaint against another, forgiving each other; as the Lord has forgiven you, so you also must forgive. And above all these put on love, which binds everything together in perfect harmony. (Col 3:12–14)

Remember those who are in prison, as though in prison with them, and those who are mistreated, since you also are in the body. (Heb 13:3)

Finally, all of you, have unity of mind, sympathy, brotherly love, a tender heart, and a humble mind. (1 Pet 3:8)

By this we know love, that he laid down his life for us, and we ought to lay down our lives for the brothers. But if anyone has the world's goods and sees his brother in need, yet closes his heart against him, how does God's love abide in him? (1 John 3:16–17)

When the church is thriving as designed, people are connected and interact in beautiful ways. Every single person is vitally needed.

These scriptures do not leave any wiggle room for silence.

FAMILY AND CHURCH MEMBERSHIP ARE NOT THE SAME

Even the concept of membership fails to capture the biblical design of the church's interconnected system. COVID-19 was a gut-punching reminder of the insufficiency of church membership. Pastors scrambled for over a year to keep their congregations together while boasting large "membership" numbers. In contrast, the relational connections between individual believers quickly became essential; the membership tally in the church database was less significant.

My dear friend and brother Johnathan Thomas, a church planter and pastor of Pacific Crest Church in Wenatchee, Washington, understood this idea well before stay-at-home orders tanked our traditional church metrics for success. Their congregation replaced the membership model for a simpler, more relational one. Johno shared his model with Common Ground Church during the pandemic (via online chat). Here are their three determinants for connection:

1. Do you know someone's name, and does that individual know your name?

2. Do you know something about their story, and do they know something about your story?

3. Have you both served together in ministry?

Anyone who can say yes to all three tenets can consider themselves connected to Pacific Crest. Simple.

Johno told me that their model increased the number of people who identified Pacific Crest as their home church. This effect occurred because Sunday attendance was not the determinant for connection. Instead, Pacific Crest made it a priority to get to know people in their city, which is why residents can say yes to all three of their connection criteria. Their guiding principle is "You can belong before you believe."[6]

A practical result of this connection model at Common Ground was that no one fell through the cracks during Covid. Instead, the people connections before Covid sustained our congregation throughout the shelter-in-place protocols and all the other difficulties of 2020.

Let me be specific—

Those in relationship with their Black pastor and his family —when our days got tough, they knew what to do!

6. Johnathan Thomas shared his concepts about church connection with me during a Zoom meeting on June 5, 2020.

So, here is what *you* should do moving forward.

DO THIS

When a brother or sister in Christ tells you that they are wounded, neglected, dismissed, mistreated, or unexplainably in pain, allow the gospel to compel you into relational action! With the four rhythms of collaboration flowing well ahead of the next inevitable racial craziness, speak intelligently on behalf of the people you love. Move quickly to their side. Bring a tissue box, sit quietly on their porch, and lament their grief. If they let you in, cool. And if they are too weak for a visit? Allow that to be okay too. Never dismiss their pain or attempt to soften their pissed-off-ness. Pray over them, and when possible, with them. Discern in the Spirit that their world got rocked; so, love them while they get their bearings. When you call on the phone and they answer it, cool. If they never pick up, fine. Let nothing stand in your way of being family. And understand that this advice comes from one Black man. If your Black friends tell you that my counsel is whack, then let that be okay too.

Now *that* is what the multiracial body of Christ needs to move forward!

I humbly conclude with a few thoughts about love and compassion.

PARABLE OF THE NEIGHBORHOOD

On April 3, 1968, two doctors met in Memphis, Tennessee, to publicly condemn the unholy silence prevalent in America and worldwide—Dr. Martin Luther King Jr. and Dr. Luke. King concluded his final sermon using a text only found in the Gospel of Luke. Commonly known today as the parable of the good Samaritan, Jesus told a fictional story to answer a self-justifying lawyer's question "And who is my neighbor?" (Luke 10:29b). At the end of the story, Jesus responded to the question with a different question:

"Which of these three, do you think, proved to be a neighbor to the man who fell among the robbers?" He said, "The one who showed him mercy." And Jesus said to him, "You go, and do likewise." (Luke 10:36–37)

The lawyer's question ("Who is my neighbor?") was his attempt to justify whom he preferred to help. Jesus' question about who was being neighborly gave a snapshot of how his followers should always respond in his kingdom. Compassionate hearts will attentively show mercy to anyone at any time.

Why?

They know that every human is created in the image of God and is a citizen of the worldwide neighborhood. So, the takeaway from Luke 10 is clear—be *less* concerned about who your neighbor is and *more* vigilant about being a neighbor!

Dr. King masterfully preached this point in his final sermon:

> And you know, it's possible that the priest and the Levite looked over that man on the ground and wondered if the robbers were still around. Or it's possible that they felt that the man on the ground was merely faking. And he was acting like he had been robbed and hurt, in order to seize them over there, lure them there for quick and easy seizure. And so the first question that the priest asked—the first question that the Levite asked was, "If I stop to help this man, what will happen to me?" But then the Good Samaritan came by. And he reversed the question: "*If I do not stop to help this man, what will happen to him?*"[7]

King's concluding and timely question ought to be answered by everyone who calls on the name of the Lord. If *you* do nothing—or say nothing—what will happen to *them*? The main issue is not about a person's lack of bravery in difficult circumstances. It is much more egregious than that. The problem is a lack of proactive fortitude to initiate love and compassion.

The wound did not come from a lack of brave White believers.

It came from a lack of you being there.

It ain't that complicated.

7. King, "Mountaintop," para. 42 (emphasis mine).

TWO KINDS OF LOVE

Admittedly, humanity's natural inclination is to love "because of":

* Because someone is kind to us, we love them.

* Because a friend sticks by you through thick and thin, you love them.

* Because someone is physically attractive, we love them.

* Because someone meets your needs or positively contributes to your life, you love them.

We all understand this kind of love. It is prevalent, and it has strings attached. It works, but it has conditions.

In contrast, the Father, Son, and Holy Spirit love us "in spite of":

* Regardless of our failings, God loves us.

* Despite my broken promises, Christ loves me.

* Notwithstanding your bitter spirit, the Holy Spirit loves you.

* In spite of our worry and lack of trust in him, he loves us.

> For while we were still weak, at the right time Christ died for the ungodly. For one will scarcely die for a righteous person—though perhaps for a good person one would dare even to die—but God shows his love for us in that while we were still sinners, Christ died for us. (Rom 5:6–8)

Reimagine what the twenty-first-century church would look like if we loved one another the way God loves us.

Consider how your reaction to others would change if you saw yourself in them.

Dream of a world (or body of believers) where silence amid a broken world turns into compassionate acts of mercy and grace.

I have those dreams—all the time.

Peace,

Avery

Appendix A

List of Interviewees and Responses to Four Questions about Collaboration

TABLE A-1: LIST OF INTERVIEWEES

Date of Interview	Name	Role	Organization	City, State	Method of Interview
July 10	Dan McClure	Former Lead Pastor	First Christian Church	Palo Alto, CA	Phone
July 11	Paul Allen Riggs	Vision and Teaching Pastor	Anthem Church	Beaverton, OR	In Person
July 11	Sudha Peethala	Lead Pastor	India International Church	Hillsboro, OR	In Person
July 12	Frank Kane	Life Community Director	Common Ground Church	Beaverton, OR	In Person
July 12	Rob Schulze	Administration and Compassion Pastor	Peninsula Bible Church	Palo Alto, CA	Phone

Date of Interview	Name	Role	Organization	City, State	Method of Interview
July 15	Larry Annes	Former Chair of Church Council	Parkside Fellowship	Beaverton, OR	In Person
July 15	Tony Huynh	Director of Disciple Making & Asian American Ministry	Village Church	Beaverton, OR	In Person
July 16	Doug Boyd	Lead Pastor	Parkside Fellowship	Beaverton, OR	In Person
July 16	Mike Harrison	Senior Pastor	Parkland Chapel	Farmington, MO	Phone
July 17	Matt Bowen	Lead Pastor	Emmaus Road	Beaverton, OR	In Person
July 17	Ed Glinden	Former Recovery Ministry Pastor	Central Peninsula Church	Foster City, CA	Phone
July 18	Daniel Estrada	Pastor	Iglesia Bautista El Buen Pastor	Beaverton, OR	In Person
July 22	Kelley Reid	Worship Pastor	Camarillo Community Church	Camarillo, CA	Phone
July 23	Bruce Fong	Professor of Pastoral Ministries and Dean	Dallas Theological Seminary Houston	Houston, TX	Phone
July 23	Reg Cox	Director	Lakewood Connects	Lakewood, CO	Phone
July 23	John Nadolski	Former Director of Church Engagement	Living Water International	Houston, TX	Phone
July 25	Dan Jocoy	Minister and Equipper	Tri-Cities Church of Christ	Myrtle Creek, OR	Phone
July 25	David Odell	Pastor	First Baptist Church	The Dalles, OR	Phone

Date of Interview	Name	Role	Organization	City, State	Method of Interview
July 25	Norm Langston	Former Pastor	First Baptist Church	Beaverton, OR	In Person
July 25	Tom Greene	Lay Teacher and Small-Group Leader	Shoreline Church	Monterey, CA	Phone
August 7	Daniel Johnson	Former College-Ministry Missionary	Josiah Ventures	Olomouc, Czech Republic	Online Chat
August 13	Jinkyu (Peter) Kim	Pastor	Global Community Church	Beaverton, OR	In Person
August 15	Paul Kroger	Executive Director	Vine & Village; Mosaic Church	Little Rock, AR	Phone
August 15	Joel King	Lead Pastor	Trinity Church of Sunnyvale	Sunnyvale, CA	Phone
August 16	Ernie Morales	Pastor of Local & Global Missions	Trinity Church of Sunnyvale	Sunnyvale, CA	Phone
August 21	Samuel Middlebrook	Former Pastor	Graceroots Community Church	Yakima, WA	Phone
August 22	Derek Chinn	Assistant Professor of Pastoral Ministries and Dean	Multnomah Biblical Seminary	Portland, OR	Phone
August 27	David Whitaker	President	Venture Church Network	Goodyear, AZ	Phone
August 28	Ikki Soma	Lead Pastor	Bayou City Fellowship	Houston, TX	Phone
August 28	Adam Paa	Care Minister	The Village Church	Flower Mound, TX	Phone

Appendix A

Date of Interview	Name	Role	Organization	City, State	Method of Interview
September 4	Jon Collins	Cofounder, Writer, and Creative Director	The Bible Project	Portland, OR	In Person
October 2	Keivan Tehrani	Global Compassion Pastor	Westgate Church	San Jose, CA	Phone

TABLE A-2: INTERVIEWEES' TOP VALUES FOR THEIR MINISTRY CONTEXT

Thirty-two participants answered the question "What are the top values for your ministry context?"[1]

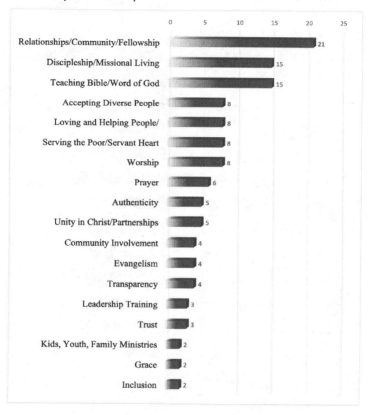

TABLE A-3: INTERVIEWEES' TOP BARRIERS TO LOCAL CHURCH COLLABORATION

Thirty-two participants answered the question "In your opinion, what are the barriers that prevent local churches from collaborating with one another?"[2]

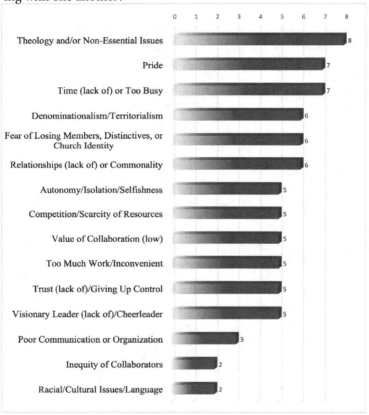

2 Other single responses included dissimilar goals and moving too fast.

TABLE A-4: INTERVIEWEES' TOP SOLUTIONS TO OVERCOME COLLABORATION BARRIERS

Thirty-two participants answered the question "What are your solutions for local churches to overcome collaboration barriers?"

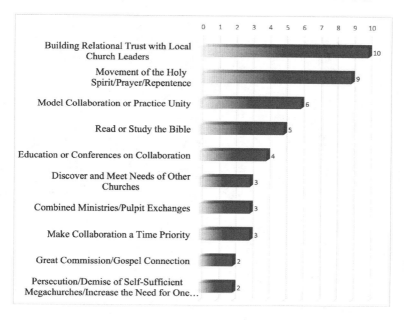

TABLE A-5: INTERVIEWEES' TOP METRICS FOR SUCCESSFUL COLLABORATION

Thirty-two participants answered the question "When local churches collaborate, how should they measure success?"[3]

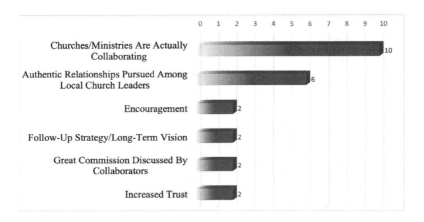

3 Other single responses included beliefs and practices reevaluated, discussing community concerns, churches redistributing power, movement of the Holy Spirit, building community relationships, spiritual transformation, agreeing on the metrics for success, and increased value placed on collaboration.

Appendix B

TABLE B: POLL OF LOCALLY OWNED COFFEE SHOPS

I asked my social media followers to name their favorite locally owned coffee shops—no national chains or drive-through shops. Below are their responses, compiled between July 2 and July 6, 2021. Perhaps one of them will become your new location for $TAB.[4]

State or Country	City or District	Coffee Shop	Website
Alaska	Ketchikan	Raven's Brew	ravensbrewcoffee.com/
Arkansas	Searcy	Midnight Oil	kibomidnightoil.com/
California	Castro Valley	Café 4	www.cvcafe4.com/
	Clovis	On the Edge	yelp.com/biz/ on-the-edge-clovis
	Fontana	Red Hill	redhillcoffeeshop.com/
	Fremont	Devout	devoutcoffee.com/
	Fresno	Frappe House	frappehouse.org/

4 Some locations may not have dine-in seating available.

State or Country	City or District	Coffee Shop	Website
	Fresno	Kuppa Joy	kuppajoy.com/
	Hanford	One Eleven	store.oneeleven.coffee/
	Los Angeles	Literati	https://www.literaticafe.com/
	Madera	Axis	https://www.axistesoro.com/
	Marina	Coffee Mia	yelp.com/biz/coffee-mia-brew-bar-and-cafe-marina
	Mountain View	Red Rock	redrockcoffee.com/
	Placerville	Totem	totemcoffeeroasters.com/
	San Francisco	Craftsman and Wolves	craftsman-wolves.com/
	San Jose	Chromatic	chromaticcoffee.com/
	San Leandro	Zocalo	zocalocoffee.com/
	San Lorenzo	Frodo Joe's	frodojoes.com/
	Santa Barbara	Handlebar	handlebarcoffee.com/
	Santa Clara	Big Mug	bigmugcoffeeroasters.com
	Santa Cruz	The Abbey	abbeycoffee.org/
	Santa Cruz	Verve	vervecoffee.com/
	Summerland	Red Kettle	redkettlecoffee.com/
	Sunnyvale	Bean Scene	beanscenecafe.com/
	Sunnyvale	Coffee and More	coffeeandmore.co/
	Tehachapi	The Coffee Mill	thecoffeemilltehachapi.com/
Colorado	Denver	The Noshery	nosherycafe.com/

State or Country	City or District	Coffee Shop	Website
	Denver	Tenn Street	tennstreetcoffee.com/
	Glenwood Springs	Deja Brew	dejabrewglenwood.com/
	Wheat Ridge	Bardo	bardocoffee.com/wheatridge
Florida	Jacksonville	Sago	sagocoffeejax.com
	Jacksonville	Setlan	setlancoffee.com
	Neptune Beach	Southern Grounds	southerngrounds.com/
Georgia	Carrollton	Gallery Row	galleryrowcoffee.com/
Idaho	Boise	Form and Function	formandfunctioncoffee.com/
	Garden City	Push and Pour	pushandpour.com/
	Grangeville	Crema	yelp.com/biz/ crema-cafe-grangeville
Illinois	Plainfield	Krema	kremacoffeehouse.com/
Minnesota	Minneapolis	Spyhouse	spyhousecoffee.com/
Ohio	Canton	Muggswigz	muggswigz.com/
Oklahoma	Morris	The Coffee Vault	thecoffeevault.business.site/
	Tulsa	Doubleshot	doubleshotcoffee.com/
	Tulsa	Shades of Brown	shadescoffee.com/
Oregon	Ashland	Noble	noblecoffeeroasting.com/
	Beaverton	Jim and Patty's	jimandpattys.com/
	Beaverton	Lionheart	lionheartcoffee.com/
	Beaverton	Thornton	thorntoncoffee.com/

State or Country	City or District	Coffee Shop	Website
	Bend	Kevista	kevistacoffee.com/
	Cannon Beach	Sleepy Monk	sleepymonkcoffee.com/
	Grants Pass	Rogue	rogueroasters.com/
	Gresham	Café Delirium	cafedelirium.com
	Hillsboro	Insomnia	insomniacoffee.co/
	McMinnville	Laughing Bean	yelp.com/biz/laughing-bean-bistro-mcminnville
	Medford	Forage	foragecoffeeco.com/
	Newberg	Chapters	chaptersbooksandcoffee.com/
	Newberg	Coffee Cottage	coffeecottage.net/
	Portland	Arbor Lodge	thearborlodge.com/
	Portland	Cathedral	cathedralcoffee.com/
	Portland	Deadstock	deadstockcoffee.com/
	Portland	Either/Or	eitherorpdx.com/
	Portland	Great North	thegreatnorthcoffee.com/
	Portland	Never	nevercoffeelab.com/
	Sisters	Sisters	sisterscoffee.com/
	Stayton	Covered Bridge	yelp.com/biz/covered-bridge-cafe-stayton
	Tigard	Jet Set	yelp.com/biz/jet-set-coffee-tigard
	Tigard	Symposium	symposiumcoffee.com/
Pennsylvania	Scranton	Northern Lights	northernlightespresso.com/

State or Country	City or District	Coffee Shop	Website
South Carolina	Greer	Barista Alley	baristaalley.com/
Tennessee	Nashville	The Well	wellcoffeehouse.com/
Texas	Granbury	Tree of Life	tolcoffee.com/
	Pasadena	Sycamore Grounds	sycamoregrounds.com
Virginia	Montross	The Art of Coffee	theartofcoffee.biz
Washington	Battle Ground	Hidden River	hiddenriverroasters.com/
	Bellevue	Dote	dailydote.com/
	Longview	Hearth	yelp.com/biz/hearth-coffee-and-cafe-longview
	Mill Creek	Spotted Cow	spotted-cow-coffee-company-106097.square.site/
	Port Orchard	Coffee Oasis	thecoffeeoasis.com/
	Port Orchard	Revive	yelp.com/biz/revive-coffee-house-and-frozen-yogurt-port-orchard
	Seattle	Hello Em Việt	yelp.com/biz/hello-em-viet-coffee-and-roastery-seattle-2
	Shoreline	Black	blackcoffeenw.com/
	Spokane	Atticus	yelp.com/biz/atticus-coffee-and-gifts-spokane
	Tacoma	Valhalla	valhallacoffee.com/
	Wenatchee	Mela	melacoffee.com/
South Korea	Seodaemun, Seoul	Potid	mangoplate.com/en/restaurants/Vr6JsLwMQ5yH
	Gwangjin, Seoul	Cafe Armoire	english.visitseoul.net/restaurants/Cafe-Armoire_/27220

State or Country	City or District	Coffee Shop	Website
Thailand	Rawai, Phuket	Hock Hoe Lee	hockhoelee.com/
	Phuket Town, Phuket	CUB House Phuket	facebook.com/ CUBhousePhuket/

In case you were curious, here are a few of my favorite coffee spots.

State or Country	City or District	Coffee Shop	Website
California	San Jose	Philz	philzcoffee.com
Oregon	Beaverton	Jim and Patty's	jimandpattys.com/
	Beaverton	La Provence, Progress Ridge	provencepdx.com/ lp-beaverton
	Portland	Caffe Umbria	caffeumbria.com
Washington	Steilacoom	Topside	topsidebargrill.com

Appendix C

Devotional Reflections for All Seven Chapters

CHAPTER 1: MIRRORS

Devotional Reflections (Individually or in Small Groups)

1. Finish these two statements:

   "I use mirrors to . . ."

   "My home church reminds me of a . . ." (analogy like family, business, hospital, social club, etc.). Would you please explain your responses (in small groups, share your explanations)?

2. Read John 17 in its entirety. Use your favorite translation plus a paraphrase like Eugene Peterson's The Message. Which verses (or words) in Jesus' prayer draw your attention? Spend five minutes highlighting them in your Bible or writing them down.

3. What are the indicators that a church is a) mirroring the relational oneness of the Father and the Son, or b) using a different mirror to measure church growth? Write your responses down (in small groups, compare lists).

4. From the previous question, in which indicators from the "first mirror" are you and your church excelling? In need of movement? What about the "second" mirror? Write your responses down (in small groups, compare lists).

5. Prayer focus: "God, help my church-growth indicators to reflect the heart of Christ."

6. Song of reflection: "Don't Pass Me By" as performed by TONE6.

CHAPTER 2: THE GOD WHO WANTS TO BE KNOWN

Devotional Reflections (Individually or in Small Groups)

1. Write down a few analogies that describe (a) your perception of God and (b) your relationship with God (in small groups, share your lists).

2. In what ways has God shown his desire to be known by you? Be as specific as possible, including dates, locations, circumstances, etc. (in small groups, share your lists).

3. Read Acts 17:16–31. Use your favorite translation plus a paraphrase like The Passion Translation. Which verses (or words) in Paul's address draw your attention? Spend five to ten minutes highlighting them in your Bible or writing them down.

4. Your current pursuit of a relationship with God is (a) active, (b) on hold, or (c) abandoned? Write down your honest introspection (in small groups, share your reflections).

5. Your current pursuit of relationships with others in Christ (same a, b, and c as above)? Write down your honest introspection (in small groups, share your reflections).

6. Prayer focus: "God, reshape my pursuit of relationships in Christ to mirror your pursuit of me."

7. Song of reflection: "Goodness of God" as performed by Cece Winans

CHAPTER 3: IMITATING THE TRINITY

Devotional Reflections (Individually or in Small Groups)

1. Write down the names of people who are (a) spiritually rooting *for* you, (b) walking *with* you, and (c) keeping you *in* their thoughts and prayers. What are the indicators of their support (in small groups, share your responses)?

2. Who are *you* spiritually (a) rooting *for*, b) walking *with*, and c) keeping *in* your thoughts and prayers? What are the indicators of your support (in small groups, share your responses)?

3. Read Deut 31:6, Isa 41:10, and 2 Cor 1:3–4. Use your favorite translation. Which verses (or phrases) draw your attention? Spend five to ten minutes highlighting them in your Bible or writing them down.

4. In what practical ways has God been (a) rooting *for* you, (b) walking *with* you, and c) living *in* you? Be as specific as possible, including dates, locations, circumstances, etc. (in small groups, share your lists).

5. Consider how your church might mirror God in your relationships with other churches in your city. Then, write down a few practical ideas (in small groups, share your thoughts).

6. Prayer focus: "Father, Son, and Spirit, align my heart to love others the way you love one another."

7. Song of reflection: "Tell Me Something I Don't Know" as performed by Acappella.

CHAPTER 4: BACK TO THE ONE

Devotional Reflections (Individually or in Small Groups)

1. Recount a time when you felt out of sync with Christ. What helped you get back to the "one"? Be as specific as possible (in small groups, share your testimonies).

2. Read Rom 8:28–39. Use your favorite translation plus a paraphrase like Peterson's The Message. Which verses (or phrases) draw your attention? Spend five to ten minutes highlighting them in your Bible or writing them down.

3. If you were visiting a new church, what indicators would convince you that they are part of the body of Christ? Spend several minutes writing them down (in small groups, share and compare your responses).

4. When visitors attend *your* church, what obvious ways can show your connection to the body of Christ? Spend several minutes writing them down (in small groups, share your indicators).

5. In what practical ways could the local churches collaboratively bless your city? Write down your dream list (in small groups, share your ideas).

6. Prayer focus: "Triune God, make your people one as you are one."

7. Song of reflection: "By Our Love" as performed by for King & Country.

CHAPTER 5: FOUR RHYTHMS OF COLLABORATION

Devotional Reflections (Individually or in Small Groups)

1. Read 1 John 3:1–3, Isa 53:1–5, and John 16:12–15. Use your favorite translation plus a paraphrase like The Passion Translation. Focus on the ways the Father, Son, and Holy Spirit demonstrate their love for you. Spend ten to fifteen minutes highlighting your Bible or writing them down.

2. Consider how the Father, Son, and Holy Spirit model the four rhythms. Then write down ways that you and your church can model him (in small groups, share your insights).

3. Pray over the four rhythms of collaboration (initiate relationships, build trust, celebrate diversity, invite inclusion). Then, write down a few ways you and your church can jump into the flow (in small groups, share your insights).

4. Take a few minutes and imagine your city filled with churches that flow in these rhythms. Then, write down what comes to mind (in small groups, share your dreams, concerns, etc.).

5. Prayer focus: "Holy Trinity, empower your children to be a public display of heaven on earth."

6. Song of reflection: "O Praise the Name" as performed by This Hope.

CHAPTER 6: ESSENTIALS AND HURDLES

Devotional Reflections (Individually or in Small Groups)

1. On a scale of 1 (extremely uncomfortable) to 10 (very comfortable), describe your experience fellowshiping or working with outside churches. Write down a couple of personal examples (in small groups, share your testimonies).

2. Write down the biggest reasons why local churches seldom partner in gospel initiatives. Give a brief explanation for each hurdle (in small groups, share your response).

3. Read Rom 1:8–12, Eph 6:18, Col 1:3–14, and 2 Tim 1:3. Use your favorite translation. Allow these passages to elevate your value of praying for the body of Christ. Spend ten to fifteen minutes highlighting your Bible or writing them down.

4. List from memory the names of local churches in your city. Commit to praying for each church at least twice in the next month. Expand your list over the same thirty days of prayer (also a small-group activity).

5. Prayer focus: "Father, stir in me a desire to pray daily for your church."

6. Song of reflection: "When We Pray" as performed by Tauren Wells.

CHAPTER 7: INTERVIEWS AND REFLECTIONS

Devotional Reflections (Individually or in Small Groups)

1. Read 1 Cor 13 in its entirety. Ask the Lord to use it to frame your thoughts about the unity of believers. Which verses (or words) capture your attention? Spend ten to fifteen minutes highlighting them in your Bible or writing them down.

2. What are your spiritual gifts or the hobbies/activities that give you joy? Pray and ask God to show you how/where to use your gift(s) to initiate relationships, build trust, celebrate diversity, and invite inclusion. Then, journal your reflections (in small groups, share them).

3. Reread the section "Twelve Recommendations" in this chapter. Are any of them actionable recommendations that resonate with your church? If so, identify them and write down some ways to put them into action (in small groups, share/compare suggestions).

4. Visit a local church's website and locate their contact page. Please spend a few minutes sending them a short, encouraging message. Let them know that a fellow believer is rooting for them in Jesus' name. Write the church's name plus the date and time you contacted them. Ask God to keep them in your prayerful heart.

5. Plan to visit a local worship service. The chances are good that you will find a service that does not conflict with your home-church gathering. Ask the Lord to increase your heart connection to the body of Christ as a result of your visit. Write down reflections from your visit (in small groups, share your experience).

6. List from memory the names of local pastors/church leaders in your city. Then, commit to praying for each of them at least

twice in the next month. Then, expand your list over the same thirty days of prayer (also a small-group activity).

7. Prayer focus: "God in heaven, show me the collaborative work that you have placed on my path."

8. Song of reflection: "Build Your Kingdom Here" as performed by Rend Collective.

Appendix D

Sample Order of Collaborative Worship Service

Here is the worship flow taken from a collaborative gathering at Grace Church in downtown Portland on May 6, 2020. Use it as a template for your own area-wide gatherings.

Welcome & Introduction
Pastor Ken Garrett, Grace Church

Song: "Our Father"
Ben and Heidi Sadler, worship leaders

Ten-Minute Message: "We Need Mercy" (Luke 18:9–14, the pharisee and publican)
Pastor Avery Stafford, Common Ground Church

Song: "Prayers of the People"

Congregational Prayer: Mercy for the Church (body of Christ) (huddle in groups and pray together)

Song: "Isaiah 6"

Congregational Prayer: Mercy for Families
(huddle in groups and pray together)

Song: "Holy Spirit"

Congregational Prayer: Mercy for Health and Well-Being
(huddle in groups and pray together)

Congregational Prayer: Mercy During Seasons of Grief
(huddle in groups and pray together)

Song: "Psalm 23"

Congregational Prayer: Mercy for the Future/Unknown

Song: "Holy, Holy, Holy"
Song: "Beautiful"

Communion/Final Blessing
Pastor Ken

Appendix E

Lyrics to "One" by Avery Stafford

"One"
Words and music by Avery Stafford
© 2003 by Avery Stafford

The anguish of Calv'ry lingered through the night
What would they do with the man called Jesus Christ?
With terror all around, He knelt in prayer for all His believers
He prayed that (chorus)

Chorus
They would all be one
They would all be one
Like the Father and the Son
Could you imagine what could be done
If they all were one
Community of one
Brothers and sisters—if they all were one?

I want my believers to live in harmony
Sharing my love among diversity
Holy Spirit, take them by the hand and keep them together—
so that (chorus)

Bridge
When will we see His answered prayer—will it be in our lifetime?
Will the children ever know we care for all His believers?
When will we be one?
So I will pray—that (chorus)

Listen to "One" by Avery Stafford on Spotify, iTunes, Pandora, YouTube, and other music-streaming services.

Bibliography

"About Denominations." World Christian Database. https://worldchristian database.org/.

"About Race." United States Census Bureau. https://www.census.gov/topics/population/race/about.html.

"Arius and Nicea." Fuller. https://www.fuller.edu/next-faithful-step/resources/arius-and-nicea/.

Barth, Karl. *Church Dogmatics*. Volume 1.1, *The Doctrine of the Word of God*. Translated by Geoffrey Bromiley. Edinburgh: T. & T. Clark, 1975.

Breen, Mike, and Scott Cockram. *Building a Discipling Culture: How to Release a Missional Movement by Discipling People Like Jesus Did*. Pawleys Island, SC: 3DM, 2009.

Brisco, Brad. "Rethinking the Missio Dei." *Missiology* (blog). Send Institute. July 10, 2018. https://www.sendinstitute.org/rethinking-the-missio-dei/.

Butler, Phill. *Well Connected: Releasing Power, Restoring Hope through Kingdom Partnerships*. Waynesboro, GA: Authentic Media, 2005.

Chinn, Derek. *1 + 1 = 1: Creating a Multiracial Church from Single Race Congregations*. Eugene, OR: Pickwick, 2012.

Cook, Jason. "The Gift of Going Second." *Gospel Coalition*, September 24, 2016. https://www.thegospelcoalition.org/article/the-gift-of-going-second/.

Dernbach, Christoph. "MacWorld Boston 1997—Steve Jobs Returns—Bill Gates Appears on Screen." *Timeline Steve Jobs* (blog). Mac History. July 19, 2008. https://www.mac-history.net/apple-history-tv/2008-07-19/macworld-boston-1997-steve-jobs-returns-bill-gates-appeares-on-screen.

DeYmaz, Mark. *Disruption: Repurposing the Church to Redeem the Community*. Nashville: Thomas Nelson, 2017.

"Do Multiracial Churches Offer Healthy Community for Non-White Attendees?" Barna Group. April 28, 2021. https://www.barna.com/research/multiracial-church/.

Dueker, Greg. "The Magnificent Spirit-Filled Seven (Acts 6:1–8)." *Our Long View* (blog). July 8, 2016. https://ourlongview.blogspot.com/2016/07/the-magnificent-spirit-filled-seven.html.

Earls, Aaron. "Small, Struggling Congregations Fill US Church Landscape." *Church Life* (blog). Lifeway Research. March 6, 2019. https://

lifewayresearch.com/2019/03/06/small-struggling-congregations-fill-u-s-church-landscape/.

Fernando, Ajith. "The Way of Unifying Passion." Lecture. July 24, 2017. Ancol Village, Jakarta, Indonesia. https://www.youtube.com/watch?v=mgOn8rgBZlY.

Fong, Bruce W. *The Wall: The Church Should Be One . . . No More Cultural or Ethnic Separation.* Scotts Valley, CA: CreateSpace, 2011.

Gladwell, Malcolm. *The Tipping Point: How Little Things Can Make a Big Difference.* Boston: Little, Brown and Company, 2000.

"Good Eats Quotes." Quotes.net. https://www.quotes.net/mquote/744961.

Gordon, Jason. "James Brown: Most Sampled Man in the Biz." Rolling Stone. December 26, 2006. https://www.rollingstone.com/music/music-news/james-brown-most-sampled-man-in-the-biz-115798/.

Greer, Peter, et al. *Rooting for Rivals: How Collaboration and Generosity Increase the Impact of Leaders, Charities, and Churches.* Minneapolis: Bethany House, 2018.

Hasegawa, Takejiro. *Matsuyama Kagami (The Matsuyama Mirror).* Japanese Fairy Tale Series 10. Translated by Kate James. Tokyo: Kobunsha, 1886. http://www.baxleystamps.com/litho/hasegawa/kagami_1886.shtml.

Henson, John M. "Watching You." Hymnary.org. https://hymnary.org/text/all_along_on_the_road_to_the_souls_true_.

"Hispanics Are the Most Eager to Get Vaccinated—but Face Obstacles." US News & World Report. May 14, 2021. https://www.usnews.com/news/health-news/articles/2021-05-14/latinos-are-most-eager-to-get-covid-vaccine-but-face-obstacles.

"History of Mt. Olivet Baptist Church." Mt. Olivet Baptist Church. August 1, 2019. https://web.archive.org/web/20180827050943/http://mtolivet.com/pages/page.asp?page_id=164749.

Holley, Perry, and Chris Goede. "3 Questions Every Follower is Asking About Their Leader." Executive Leadership Podcast 5. The John Maxwell Co. May 15, 2018. https://corporatesolutions.johnmaxwell.com/podcast/executive-leadership-podcast-5-3-questions-every-follower-is/.

"How to Create a Collaborative Culture." Atlassian. https://www.atlassian.com/work-management/project-management/project-execution/collaborative-culture.

Hunter, James Davison. *To Change the World: The Irony, Tragedy, and Possibility of Christianity in the Late Modern World.* Oxford: Oxford University Press, 2010.

Jefferson, Thomas, et al. "Declaration of Independence: A Transcription." National Archives. https://www.archives.gov/founding-docs/declaration-transcript.

Jobs, Steve. "Macworld Boston 1997: The Microsoft Deal." Lecture. August 6, 1997. Bayside Expo Center, Boston. https://www.youtube.com/watch?v=WxOp5mBY9IY.

Johnson, Darrell W. *Experiencing the Trinity*. Vancouver, BC: Regent College Publishing, 2002.

Kanigel, Rachele. "White, White." The Diversity Style Guide. https://www.diversitystyleguide.com/glossary/white-white/.

King, Martin Luther, Jr. "Interview on 'Meet the Press.'" The Martin Luther King, Jr. Research and Education Institute. April 17, 1960. https://kinginstitute.stanford.edu/king-papers/documents/interview-meet-press.

———. "Martin Luther King's Final Speech: 'I've Been to the Mountaintop'— The Full Text." ABC News. April 3, 2013. https://abcnews.go.com/Politics/martin-luther-kings-final-speech-ive-mountaintop-full/story?id=18872817.

Leander, Brian. "7 Key Characteristics of Diversity-Oriented Churches." *Leading Ideas* (blog). Lewis Center for Church Leadership. June 14, 2017. https://www.churchleadership.com/leading-ideas/7-key-characteristics-diversity-oriented-churches/.

Letham, Robert. *The Holy Trinity in Scripture, History, Theology, and Worship.* Phillipsburg, NJ: P. & R., 2004.

"Light Up the City." https://www.lightupthecity.org/team.

Lin, Kimberly. "Narcissus Myth: Early Poets and the Ancient Story." Historic Mysteries. January 7, 2018. https://www.historicmysteries.com/narcissus-myth-version-poets/.

Loritts, Bryan (@DrLoritts). "Family and friendship are not synonymous. Your family is who you are responsible for. You don't choose family. You choose friends. Churches are families." Twitter, July 15, 2021, 4:50 p.m. https://twitter.com/DrLoritts/status/1415821062177185800.

Lovett, Ian. "'Our Lord Isn't Woke.' Southern Baptists Clash over Their Future." *Wall Street Journal*, June 11, 2021. https://www.wsj.com/articles/our-lord-isnt-woke-southern-baptists-clash-over-their-future-11623439486.

Mackie, Timothy. "What is the Shema?" *Learn What the "Shema" Is* (blog). The Bible Project. February 18, 2017. https://bibleproject.com/blog/what-is-the-shema/.

McGavran, Donald. *Bridges of God: A Study in the Strategy of Missions.* Eugene, OR: Wipf & Stock, 2005.

"Musical Dictionary." The Online Metronome. https://theonlinemetronome.com/musical-dictionary.

Pauw, Amy Plantinga. *The Supreme Harmony of All: The Trinitarian Theology of Jonathan Edwards.* Grand Rapids: Eerdmans, 2002.

Pruitt, Sarah. "Here Are 6 Things Albert Einstein Never Said." History.com. September 20, 2018. https://www.history.com/news/here-are-6-things-albert-einstein-never-said.

Ramirez, Lucas, and Mike DeVito. *Designed for More: Unleashing Christ's Vision for Unity in a Deeply Divided World.* Nashville: FaithWords, 2018.

Raymond, Dave. "How Churches Can Work Together for Mission." Church Collaboration. http://www.churchcollaboration.com/default.html.

Reardon, JoHannah. "The Nicene and Apostles' Creeds: A Close Look at These Two Creeds Helps Define What Christians Believe." Christianity Today. July 30, 2008. https://www.christianitytoday.com/biblestudies/articles/churchhomeleadership/nicene-apostles-creeds.html.

Reed, Eric. "Corporate Governance: What Does It Mean?" *TheStreet* (blog), October 30, 2018. https://www.thestreet.com/markets/corporate-governance/what-is-corporate-governance-14761397.

Reeves, Michael. *Delighting in the Trinity: An Introduction to the Christian Faith*. Downers Grove, IL: InterVarsity, 2012.

Richard, Matt. "Great Commission, Great Commandment Not Same." *Sidney Herald*. March 17, 2012. https://www.sidneyherald.com/community/religion/great-commission-great-commandment-not-same/article_3336b186-707e-11e1-95a8-0019bb2963f4.html.

Rowling, J. K. "The Mirror of Erised: J. K. Rowling's Thoughts." Wizarding World. August 10, 2015. https://www.wizardingworld.com/writing-by-jk-rowling/the-mirror-of-erised.

Sanders, Fred. *The Deep Things of God: How the Trinity Changes Everything*. 2nd ed. Wheaton, IL: Crossway, 2017.

Sproul, R. C. "The Athanasian Creed." Ligonier. https://www.ligonier.org/learn/articles/athanasian-creed/.

Stafford, Tim. "The Father of Church Growth." *Christianity Today* 30.3 (February 21, 1986) 19. https://www.christianitytoday.com/ct/1986/february-21/father-of-church-growth-over-past-50-years-few-have.html.

Stigile, Ryan. "Would Jesus Want Your Church to Be Run Like a Business?" *Leadership and Management* (blog). TonyMorganLive. June 21, 2015. https://tonymorganlive.com/2015/06/21/church-business/.

"The Tuskegee Timeline." Centers for Disease Control and Prevention. https://www.cdc.gov/tuskegee/timeline.htm.

"The Untouchables (1987)—Sean Connery: Jim Malone." IMDb. https://www.imdb.com/title/tt0094226/characters/nm0000125.

"What Is Diversity and Inclusion?" Global Diversity Practice. https://globaldiversitypractice.com/what-is-diversity-inclusion/.

Williams, Rowan. *On Augustine*. London: Bloomsbury Continuum, 2016.

"You Talkin' to Me?" IGN. https://www.ign.com/lists/movie-moments/4.